Dads' Day 2011

The Master (an
of Renovations - you
can now look back

Vive la Rénovation!

Building a life in France

by

Trevor Morris

on this adventure -
and WRITE about it!

Published by Trevor Morris
La Lauressie
82250
Laguépie
France
www.vivelarenovation.com

Cover and inside illustrations by Patrick Lewis
www. patricklewis.co.uk

Designed and printed by Marquee Print
www.marqueeprint.com

To Sue,
I dedicate this book, my life, my love ...

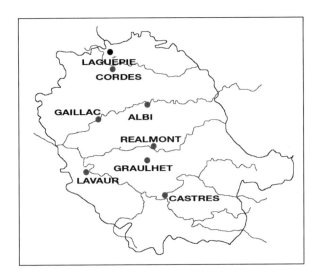

Region of The Aveyron and The Viaur

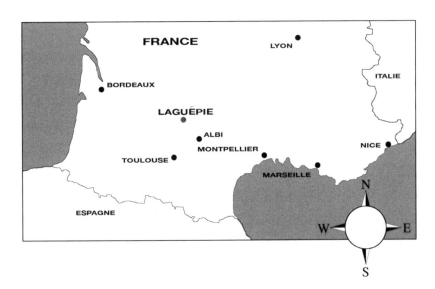

Foreword & Acknowledgements

It is rare that a journey is unaccompanied or unsupported. This journey, chronicled over 3 years of articles is no exception.

As with all journeys, mine began with inspiration. The inspiration came in the form of a somewhat irrational desire to leave behind comfort and stability for an unknown life in a foreign country. For this, I have to thank my parents, my mother and my late father, who encouraged me as a teenager to visit France on student exchanges.

They began a smouldering fire, which was later stoked by our now sadly deceased neighbour Geoff Tuckfield and his family of Charlton Down in Dorset. His generosity with the whiskey bottle and encouragement to join his son and daughter-in-law, Helen and Les, down in the south west of France gave us the aiming point that we needed.

A chance conversation with Dave Murdock, the editor of the Dorset Echo newspaper (www.dorsetecho.co.uk) gave me the platform to air my observations about the way of ex-pat life, the difficulties, the joys and also an occasional outlet to vent my spleen. For his faith in me I am grateful.

Along the way, the journey would not have been complete without the cast and crew. My clients, people I have met, those I have worked with, friends, and a fair overlap in between. Too numerous to mention individually, their presence has been invaluable in so many ways and I thank each and every one of them for it.

The creation of a book requires help from so many sources. I thank Marquee Print (www.marqueeprint.com) for their help and know how. Patrick Lewis (www.patricklewis.co.uk), illustrator and friend, for his creative artwork for the cover design and inside illustrations. Joe Biro (www.birodesign.com) for designing and building the website. French entrée (www.frenchentree.com/tarn-aveyron) for featuring and publicising my articles.

Finally, none of this would have been possible without Sue and the cats. Sue has been beside me literally and figuratively all the way while the cats have been mainly under my feet. For her patient editing, re-editing and editing again, I have nothing but praise.

Winter 2002

Starting Over

We had just hit that point, as we approached forty, when for the first time in our lives we were not struggling to keep our heads above water. I had got my one-man building business established, Sue was on a good grade at the local authority and we were set up in a lovely apartment in the Dorset countryside...

So what did we decide to do? Well, give it all up and move to France to start a new life. It was decided. I would wind up the business, Sue would give in her notice, and we would let the apartment out. On the vague promise of some work and the loan of a holiday gîte from a friend of a friend, we would head off into the unknown - south west France, to be precise - with a small amount of money in the bank, in the middle of winter.

Everything was meticulously planned, down to the last detail. I was to look after the bills, the new tenants, the transport, the money, the contacts for work etc. Sue was to pack the clothes and sort out the cats. I throw in the word cats, as if cats are an incidental. Unfortunately, they are not, at least not in our house. I am approximately fifth in the pecking order (behind three cats, in order of seniority) and liable to slip to a lower point at any time.

A date was set, a van was hired, tickets for the channel tunnel booked. Tenants were helped to move in and we were off. I drove the hire van up to Croydon to stay the night with my brother while Sue followed in the Escort van with her precious cargo of cats safely packed in their boxes in the back. It is worth noting at this point, that I had packed everything that we owned into a high top Transit, tools, furniture, the lot. When I had finished, you could not have even fitted a spare tea bag in the back of the van.

We arrived safely in Croydon to the news that the Tunnel was shut and that there were huge delays on the motorways. We were due to catch the early train and make the long drive in one hit the next day, delays were not in the plan. A quick phone call to the helpline allayed our fears. A Chinese takeaway was ordered and we had our first hitch.

My brother was planning to come down with us, driving the hire van with his girlfriend, while we drove the Escort. He would then bring the van back to the UK for us, saving me a couple of trips. That's what brothers are for. He turned to his girlfriend and said, "Have you got the passports?". I looked at Sue, and she at me. The question did not really need asking. We both knew it and we both knew the answer. I could have cried, after locking all that furniture in the back of the van like a huge Chinese puzzle and driving it one hundred and fifty miles, I would rather have eaten one of my own arms than have to start looking for those passports. But unpacking was the only option if we were to pass customs. I consoled myself with the idea that eight in the evening was better than four in the morning, and so with a heavy heart I wandered out into the black and heavy Croydon air. I recalled, I thought, that the passports were in the filing cabinet and that this was not far from the back. I opened the rear doors to the sound of assorted last minute items such as bins, mops etc hitting the floor. I pulled the duvet out and looked with dread at the mattress that was stuffed across the top holding it all in place, wondering how I would get it all in again. In the gloom I spotted a corner of the filing cabinet. My heart leapt, but I was ready for disappointment. I moved some more items out of the way. There was a one in four chance that it would be pointing the right way. There was a God! the drawer was right in front of me and the passports were exactly where they should have been. If I knew how to do a somersault in mid air, I would have done several, planes going in to Gatwick could see the grin on my face.

A bleary eyed start was made the next day, customs decided to have a look inside the van, tried to open one door, saw the carnage and tried to slam it shut again. It took three of them and a dented door before it could be described as being shut. We drove 600 miles, with copious stops for coffee and toilets - and litter tray breaks for the cats.

At 11pm that night we walked across the threshold of the holiday gîte that we had arranged to rent for the winter. The last couple of hours of the journey had been in the driving rain on single lane carriageways that went up hill and down dale, with progress down to a snail's pace. All three cats and Sue were howling for a soft bed by this time. I won't bother mentioning the mad lorry driver who must have been watching the film 'Duel' the night before and tried several times to run me off the road.

As we fell gladly into our bed that night, we wondered what our new lives in France would have in store for us. How easy it would be to find work, how the cats would like it - and there was also the fact that Sue was running low on fags...

Twenty Fags and a Kitten Please

Sue went shopping with her friend the other day. Now, there is a sentence to reflect upon, the sort that will strike fear into the stoutest male heart. It is fraught with all kinds of dangerous worst-case / best-case scenarios.

Perhaps they will have found nothing to buy, in which case the bank balance is intact; but the happiness bubble has been displaced by a dark cloud of gloom because the shops have nothing to sell, the clothes are too small, the bum too big and life has generally lost its lustre.

The other possibility is two heavily laden females struggling with bags that it would take a team of five porters to carry to the door. In which case the bank account has taken a critical hit, but the home is a happy and congenial place to spend a little time.

They had spent the day in Gaillac, our local town which is roughly similar in size to Dorchester but with not as many shops. I returned home that Thursday evening not having a clue what to expect.

The first bad sign was that Helen was still with Sue. Moral support or a united front? Sue had her back to me when I walked in and then turned to expose a tiny grey kitten.

"I didn't want to save it, she made me. I would have left it, it was going to die. Do you hate it? Are you really angry?"

What to do? Throw the kitten outside and demand that my dinner be placed on the table? I offered to make a cup of tea while I found out the story.

In Gaillac, Sue had gone into the tabac to top up her supply of fags. Outside the tabac was a group of people looking at a small kitten shivering and cowering under a car. Sue decided to be brave and look the other way, having heard stories of other ex-pats filling their homes with numerous waifs and strays.

Inside the shop, the shopkeeper with the obligatory Gaulloise clamped in the corner of his mouth, it is still acceptable to smoke in shops over here, it is in fact compulsory in some, explained in broken English, helped by Helen's translation that the kitten was lost.

As soon as he started his story he obviously sensed that he had two live ones "Thees cat 'e die quick, in one hour, car, boom." He explained, making a frightened cat face and then miming a car splatting it.

He knew that he had made a sale, handed over a couple of packets of menthe cigarettes and lifetime ownership of a small cat. He promised to put a notice up in the shop window and waved goodbye. We have not seen a lost and found sign. We suspect that he just went upstairs to fetch a bottle of Pastis to celebrate his good fortune in finding a victim for the 'He'll be dead if you don't save him' routine.

I explained that we did not have room in a tiny gîte for yet another cat, that we would have to take it back so that it could fend for itself on the mean streets of Gaillac. Then I folded. Monty had arrived.

Digging Foundations

The first construction project of the New Year has just arrived, rousing me from the semi retirement that has shown no signs of happening. It is an old grange (barn) that has at various times housed assorted livestock and up to three families. The families bit is important, because in this area of France they are no longer giving planning permission to convert granges into residences unless you can prove that they have been inhabited in the past by bipeds with at least rudimentary language skills.

The job has happened upon me by a sequence of fortuitous events. I already knew the owners, an English couple with a small child. They had planned to have the conversion done by a French builder while they were working away on a contract in Kuwait. The talk of war put paid to that, so the husband has decided to stay in his airline job. The devis (quote) from the Frenchman was quite high, so the airline man decided that, seeing as his job affords him a lot of time off, he would like to try and take on some of the work himself. Not having enough time, skills or practical experience to do it all, he needed help.

This worked out nicely, given that the work that I had come out here to do for an English builder had fallen through, due to a change of his personal circumstances. So a visit was made, a plan discussed, drawings perused and a deal done.

The grange is a classic example of its type, stone-built with Mediterranean-style clay tiles on a low pitched roof. It is, however in a pitiful state and is nothing short of a ground-upwards restoration. In fact, even the ground will not be remaining, as we are excavating it to install underfloor heating. The restoration is to be sympathetic to the local area, using local wood and stone wherever practical and preserving those little historical features such as small stone sinks with bulls' eye openings above that can so easily be lost in an over-enthusiastic refurbishment.

I have just completed the first and most important phase of the work, which was to travel the area talking to everybody who has carried out restorations, bending their ears, making a nuisance of myself and hopefully finding the best sources for materials - which to use, which to avoid and what mistakes to learn from. A local electrician and a local plumber have been engaged and are ready to roll. The plumber goes by the unlikely name of Jose Fernandez but declares himself to be as French as croissants.

In order to carry out the work I have had to register with the local Chambre de Métiers, (broadly similar to a chamber of commerce) after first applying for a residency permit which could not be obtained without registration as an Artisan, which could not be obtained without a residency permit ....

The cycle was finally broken by a reasonable command of French and good old-fashioned stubborn English politeness that not even the walls of Jericho could withstand. Now that my papers have arrived we are about to break the soil and take the first steps on what may be a very long road.

*

Winds of Change

The last week in February has followed true to the old maxim that is used to describe March in the UK. It came in like a lion and went out meekly like a lamb. On Monday the wind started to pick up and blow things around the site. By Tuesday it was blowing so hard that it was becoming difficult to stand up. The wind was blowing the water straight out of the buckets that I was filling. I had to abandon work on the front of the building and work on the lee side. It continued unabated until Thursday night, the only consolation being that it was blowing up from Africa and pushing the cold weather away. After four days of constant wind it was easy to see why in Provence the Mistral wind makes people lock their doors and refuse to go outside - and in extreme circumstances prompts them to take the ultimate step. I'm not trying to say that it was that bad, but it was pretty unpleasant.

Friday morning was like the day after a wild party. There were bits of tree, tiles and rubbish strewn across the roads - but it was calm. The sun broke through, fleeces were jettisoned and T-shirts became the order of the day. People were wandering about looking almost bemused.

Apparently this is the norm. The wind blows the cold away and the temperature shoots up by about ten degrees. The trees have already started to blossom in the last couple of days. We were even encouraged to play a game of outdoor table tennis on Saturday afternoon.

On the home front, Monty, the kitten that Sue got free with twenty fags, has not been developing normally. After exhaustive examinations and opinions from various non-experts we came to the conclusion that he was not much of a boy. In fact, he was a bit of a girl. This was confirmed by a trip to the vet's. You know you are in the sticks when you share a waiting room with a lamb and other assorted farmyard animals. Monty had to be renamed Milly but has settled perfectly well to her new role as china breaker and curtain slasher.

The gendarmes paid us a visit to confirm the arrival of our cartes de séjour (residency permits), I was out at work and Sue was on her own when two handsome young men in uniforms with real guns came a-calling. She seemed rather too comfortable with this situation. Unfortunately, they spoke no English and Sue's French is still rather shaky. It seemed they wanted to know my mother's maiden name for their records. Sue tried to explain that as my mother had been married three times it was a little difficult to keep track of her name at the moment, let alone what it once was. It seems that after much laughter, nods and winks the local gendarmerie were able to deduce that I am the son of a Bohemian mother who leads a debauched life with three men. I hope they don't think that this is normal for English women, but they did seem keen to come back next week.

Spring 2003

The Thrill of the Chasse

It is Sunday and the Chasse (local hunters) are out in force again. A whole bunch of them turn up in battered white vans, abandoning them all over the road somewhere close to the most recent sighting of a sanglier (wild boar).

Out here on the edges of the Gresigne (one of the largest oak forests in Europe), the Chasse are pretty much a law unto themselves. They close roads and brandish rifles in the direction of all and sundry. They bear no relation to their Barbour-clad, shotgun-toting cousins across the Channel. These guys are dressed head to toe in brown leather and camouflage fatigues and tote rifles that fire heavy duty bullets. Apparently, if you tried to shoot a sanglier with a shotgun you would merely irritate it - not ideal, as they are midway between the size of a pig and a small horse and bad-tempered even before being specifically irritated.

The Chasse can be seen out and about twice a week. They are surprisingly easy to spot, in spite of the heavy use of camouflage because they all wear vivid fluorescent baseball caps. This seemed like a weak link in the whole camouflage thing to me, so I asked one of the locals about it. He replied that they wore the hats so that they could identify each other and be seen. I pointed out that if they could see each other with ease then the sanglier might be able to spot them as well. He laughed at my naivety, "The sanglier is colour-blind, of course he can't see the hats." I laughed as well, at my stupidity, wanting to ask: "If the damn thing is colour-blind why go out dressed like extras from Rambo when you could skip into the forest in a pink tutu with matching canary yellow accessories and still be just as well hidden?" Discretion being the better part of valour, and understanding the Gallic predisposition towards uniform at the slightest excuse, the question went unasked.

I had to ask, though, about their methods. Apparently they form a large circle around the sighted animal and close in on it. I was starting to see a flaw but my question was pre-empted. "They are only allowed to shoot outwards from the circle." Which is probably fine in theory, if you all walk at the same speed, a problem borne out by the frightening numbers of Chasse killed annually - around 28 last year. Perhaps the three-hour break at the lodge for lunch doesn't help: sanglier washed down by gallons of cheap red wine before re-arming for the afternoon session.

If you are out walking around here on a Sunday afternoon, it is probably safer to wear the big fur coat than that old combat jacket and baseball cap.

A Year in Bosnia

The barn conversion is fully under way: full steam ahead. We are engaged in making what was a perfectly viable barn into a roofless shell full of holes. The Mad Island monkeys - apparently this is how the Germans refer to the Brits, it does seem to describe us rather well - have dug up floors, made openings for new windows, built new walls and generally made a mess.

The Mad Island monkeys in this case are myself and Les, the owner, who is an airline pilot and lends a hand when he is off-duty. The building is presently at its lowest point. It looks like hell, but it is just about to improve in leaps and bounds.

The French former owner lives across the road. We see him looking at us and laughing to himself that somebody has spent an insane amount of money on a derelict building that is uninhabitable. For the same amount of money Les could have had a nice rendered villa like the one that the Frenchman owns and the majority of the French still aspire to.

The vision of hell has had a welcome boost in the shape of the cut stone for the door and window surrounds that has just arrived. It is quarried near Cordes (a beautiful medieval bastide town) by an Englishman. It was supposed to be ready about six weeks ago but the stone beds have been frozen (nobody mentioned the possibility of sub-zero temperatures stopping play in the South of France). I had prepared one opening ready to be filled, was told the delay would be a few days and so started another. This continued until the barn looked like a Swiss cheese.

It was such a great feeling to start building the sides of doors and windows back up and see the barn begin to look like the kind of place you could live in. The stones are numbered and fit together quite simply, apart from being indecently heavy. The only confusion was when I fitted the first window. I laid the stones out on the floor, and they were numbered D1-3 and G1-3. I thought this was strange as I hadn't seen A, B, C or E and F. It wasn't until window number three, that the penny finally dropped - D & G stands for droite and gauche (right and left). Fairly obvious when you think about it.

Our pile of rubble outside continues to grow, hiding us from the gaze of the neighbours who wonder what sort of place England must be if the inhabitants would rather travel several hundred miles to live in this sort of hovel. For the moment, the idyll of 'A year in Provence' is obscured by a façade somewhat closer to 'A year in Bosnia', but we shall overcome.

Estate Agents

Our current landlord has had the dubious honour of playing host to a stream of Immobiliers (estate agents) this week. They have all heard the calling of his imminent divorce and are ready to feast like vultures on the corpse of the shattered dream.

It is interesting to note that, apparently, 70 per cent of Brits get divorced within the first five years out here. A lot of people seem to move abroad in the hope that their domestic problems will fade away. Instead, they have the same problems but in a different place. We have met quite a few of these Immobiliers as they have wandered through the gîte that we are staying in, fascinatingly various in character: bottle blonde ex-pat Brits, flash guys in fast cars and overweight Frenchmen with huge moustaches. They have all had one thing in common naturally - they all want their five per cent. Our landlord,who wants about £500,000 for the place that we are staying in, says that they won't negotiate the percentage at all. It makes you realise how warm and fluffy those estate agents are in the UK. You could probably get them down to one percent on a sale like this.

One of the immobiliers is a local chap that we have met as we have been out and about looking around for a property to buy. He conducts his whole business out of the back of his car: No office, no computer just a battered old Peugeot 205 with a nicotine-yellow interior. His face has the red bloom of a seasoned boozer and when he smiles he exposes a fine row of blackened teeth. He favours nylon for his shirts, which doesn't mix well with the ever dangling cigarette. I'm sure that he will end up shrink-wrapped before long. Rumour has it that his speciality is calling round to widows who are not far from their last breath and signing them up before anybody else gets a sniff at disposing of their estate. I suspect that his biggest problem in life is how to climb on to his bed. The mattress must be nearly touching the ceiling from all the piles of notes underneath it. At five per cent a deal and no overheads you can't go too far wrong.

Our unfortunate landlord has been suffering from stress as a result of the imminent divorce and this has manifested itself in the shape of boils, the most noticeable of which was on his nose. He was discussing the sale with the immobilier, who did not agree with our landlords' valuation of the property. He set it at twenty per cent less, told him that he didn't appear to own all the land on his deeds and kept staring at the boil. In the end he could contain himself no more and pointed his pencil at the offending boil:
"You know what that is, don't you?"
"Yes, it is a boil." "No, you are mistaken, that is cancer."
At this point our landlord exploded, "You come round here, tell me my property is worth a hundred grand less, tell me I don't own my own land, that I have cancer and you still want five percent?!" He shrugged, lit another cigarette and extended his hand, "Is it a deal?"

Roofing

If you have two people who are terrified of heights, what is the worst job that you can give them? Putting the scaffolding around the spire of Salisbury Cathedral is pretty bad, but not as bad as our own worst nightmare: refurbishing the roof. After receiving astronomical quotes from French contractors who might or might not have been able to do the work some time this year or maybe next, it was with a heavy heart that the bullet was bitten.

Monday was D Day. The forecast was looking good for the week, the sun came out and the temperature gauge went flying up to the mid-20s. It was with no small sense of trepidation that I took my first few hesitant steps up on the roof. Once up there it was not so bad. The biggest fear was not so much falling off as falling through a rotten board.

The roofs in this region are the classic Roman style of interlocking flute- shaped tiles: Two rows of valleys with a crest bridging them. A fabulously simple design that is fully waterproof and not held down by a single nail. The plan was to re-use the old tiles, use new ones in the valleys where they can't be seen and put the old ones back over the top after laying down an insulating membrane. The biggest problem was that the insulating membrane is like a space blanket (the kind of thing they wrap people in after the London marathon): it is thin but covered in aluminium foil on both sides. This is great to reflect heat back in winter and heat off in summer, but it is damn shiny. Picture us both crawling around on our hands and knees, blinded, looking for the hammer and nails and trying not to fall off the edges. Having got the insulation battened down and a few tiles on the roof, Les declared that he had to go back to work, flying crates backwards and forwards across the Far East. "I'll be back in 10 days." I looked at the stack of tiles on the ground waiting to go up and all the old ones to be replaced up in the high place. "But, but." I blubbered. "You'll be okay, Trev." He said with a smile, and left.

The next day was all hands to the pumps, Les' father Geoff, a sprightly septuagenarian was pulled in to transport tiles to the bottom of the scaffold. He was assisted by our young French neighbour, Cedric, aged nine, who doesn't go to school on a Wednesday. I seemed to have the youngest and the oldest apprentices in the Tarn. The lovely bikini clad Sue was installed on the roof in charge of cleaning up the old tiles.

The team worked like a dream and we broke the back of it in one big day. Cedric drank tea like an Anglais, Geoff kept the whip cracked on us and Sue got a wonderful tan. I couldn't help wondering what the Health and Safety Executive would have made of it. One labourer too young to work, one too old to work and one with a cleavage. Only in France!

Marseille

Marseille, one of the largest French ports on the Mediterranean, it conjures up images of smoky portside cafes full of hairy tattooed sailors and painted prostitutes looking like Marlene Dietrich, in striped shirts with pencil skirts and berets. Or is that just me? Anyway, I was more than delighted when Les announced that he had bought a set of antique Indian doors in Dubai and was having them shipped to France. They were coming to Marseille and we were to go and pick them up from the bonded warehouse.

The day before we were due to pick them up Les was to fly in to Paris from Hong Kong. Unfortunately there was a French air traffic controllers' strike. Over here it can be similar to living in 1970s England; the French love nothing so much as a good strike. So Les had to land in Brussels and catch a train to Paris and down to Toulouse. This would have been okay if he hadn't had to get from one train station to another in Paris via the Metro: This in turn would have been okay if a light-fingered Moroccan hadn't lifted his wallet with £500 in cash, all his credit cards and his driving licence. A disillusioned and slightly seething Les returned late that night. I went ahead and hired the van, even though it meant that I would have to do all the driving for the 1,000km round trip and Les would have to navigate as he wouldn't be insured to drive without his licence. This should have been okay, as he used to be a navigator on Tornadoes before he flew them.

We set off early the next morning with a packed lunch, Les dreaming of his doors and me dreaming of the Marlene Dietrich look-alikes (don't tell Sue!). We made excellent time and were soon crossing the plains of The Carmague, we dissected the ongoing war and damned all pick pockets to an eternity of watching reruns of 'Are You Being Served' while being beaten with a blunt instrument.

Les had directions to the warehouse and had been assured that they did not close for the obligatory two-and-a-half hour lunch. As we entered the city outskirts I was getting a little disillusioned: it looked nothing like I had imagined, in fact it looked a bit like a sprawling Portsmouth. The navigating was going well: we found gate three, the starting point for the detailed directions, but from this point on the directions may as well have been written in ancient Greek. They seemed to bear no relation to anything that was actually going on around us.

We made a couple of circuits and then stopped to consult some security guards. "You must go and buy a coffee." One of them said. "I'm lost, not thirsty." I explained. "If you buy a coffee, you can ask the café owner." "Is he likely to know this address?" I asked. The guard shrugged and we drove off. We tried to call the warehouse and, surprise, surprise, it was after midday, nobody was answering the phone. We then drove around and around the centre of Marseille asking people for directions and getting nowhere fast. As luck would have it, we drove past the port authority, which was still open. If anybody would know where a bonded warehouse was, they would.

We parked and marched into reception. A young girl was at the desk, flirting with a couple of security guards who were plying her with cigarettes and smiles. After waiting for a polite five minutes I cut into the love match and asked for help. The look in her eye told me that I was not the sort she wanted to flirt with and could I please push off. I persevered, a pretence was made of trying to look at a map and we were sent on our way.

Desperate, we got back in the van and continued driving. We drove past a clump of lorry drivers and I had a brainwave: lorry drivers know where they are going. I slammed the brakes on, jumped out and approached a guy with a huge gunfighter moustache and a belly to match. My question sparked a furious debate, with half a dozen drivers offering different ideas of where it was, arms were flailing and voices raised. "Follow me." the gunfighter declared. I asked him which vehicle was his. He pointed to the biggest lorry I had ever seen. In disbelief, I climbed back in the van and followed 25 tons of articulated lorry through the back roads of Marseille until he finally delivered us to the front door of the warehouse. He double parked and got out to show us the building; we gave him a couple of bottles of beer to keep his belly in shape and thanked him profusely.

It was still lunchtime so we had an hour to kill, " What is in the lunch bag, Les?" "Cheese and tomato sandwiches," he said, delving into the bag for the build-your-own ingredients. "Except Helen has forgotten to put in the butter and the cheese."

"So that'll be tomato sandwiches then." I said, just a little disappointed. It was true that we had met a really helpful Frenchman who had restored our faith in human nature, but as for Marlene Dietrich...

Bread 'n' Cheese

Who would have thought it! After the best part of 20 years of cheese sandwiches every day at work, I move to France, the home of the two-hour lunch, wine, bread and cheese, and what do I miss? You guessed it, bread and cheese.

Don't get me wrong, the French do make some damn fine cheeses. Their fromage de chèvre (goats cheese) melts in the mouth, and a good quality Roquefort takes some beating, but the problem is (and this is the bit that sounds like heresy): Most of their cheeses are a bit bland. Nice texture, but not a lot of taste going on.

The closest they get to a cheddar is a Cantal vieux (old), and that is not old enough to even make you wince. I miss those mature cheddar cheeses that first make you wrinkle your nose and then start to curl your toes before making your eyes water - something with a bit of bite. We have tried buying from the markets - better than the supermarket but still not good enough. The final solution seems to be to get my friend's father, who comes over from the UK regularly, to smuggle us in a couple of pounds of cheddar at a time. He'll have a hard time explaining that one if he gets stopped by customs.

The other surprise problem is the bread. You cannot get better bread than a fresh baked baguette - it is sublime, but it has a shelf life and sometimes the shelf life expires as you walk out of the shop. On a sunny day it will be like chewing on a brick by the time you get home and there is no hope of it being any good the next day. If you try to make a sandwich out of it, you will end up with a jaw like Schwarzennegger and all the moisture drawn up out of your socks. A fresh baguette has to be eaten there and then. Your best bet is taking a seat in the boulangerie and chowing down before you leave.

At the other end of the spectrum, the French sell sliced bread nowadays - English or American style. The wrappers are different, but the bread tastes the same. We bought one of these loaves and it got forgotten. After about a week I found it in the cupboard. I was just about to launch it when I stopped to look at the sell-by-date. It still had about three weeks left - this stuff has the shelf life of an Egyptian mummy. You could take a slow boat to China and your butties would still be fresh when you got there. You could happily eat your sandwiches while your mates who had been so proud of their baguettes would have been starving since well before the Suez Canal. At the end of the day, the French might come second place to the English country farmhouse in the cheese stakes, but the English farmhouse is left standing at the gate when it comes to making a drop of wine. The Brits don't even come close and after a couple of glasses, that stale baguette and that old lump of cheese in the back of the fridge become possibly one of the best meals on this planet.

Le Box

If you thought British television was bad, you should try watching the TV over here. I was never much of a fan of television in the UK, but I do find myself drawn to watching some of the French programmes. They supply some of the same old dross as you get back home; French versions of Who Wants to be a Millionaire, The Weakest Link and even Countdown - with look-a-like presenters, scary as that seems. I only watch them for their educational value of course.

The programmes that really get my attention are the news and weather reports. This is in no small part due to their being hosted by female presenters who take considerably more care in their appearance than their British counterparts. The French presenter has beautifully coiffed hair, much jewellery and looks dressed for a night out - she doesn't look as if she has just done the school run and a load of washing.

Having said that, they do sometimes make serious fashion gaffes. Many is the evening that we have started to watch the weather screaming out: 'She can not be serious, that A-line skirt is atrocious and she should not wear cut-off sleeves with those arms.' Even when they get it wrong, they seem to do it with a style that us Brits have never mastered.

After viewing the news, followed by many more adverts than you get in the UK and often featuring naked women (obligatory if you are to sell any product that cleans), we may well watch the evening film. They do put on the odd French classic such as Monsieur Hulot's Holiday, but for the most part they are American blockbusters. My French allows me to follow a fair part of the action but the dialogue is often too fast so we have taken to bringing up the Teletext sub-titles. This is great for learning new words.

The other favourite on those long winter nights is the video or DVD. We have revisited every video we have ever owned, including no less than 57 old episodes of The Professionals. Sue has a bit of a penchant for men with dodgy hairstyles driving Ford Capris and has just talked me into allowing her to but the complete set on DVD from Amazon. The reasoning was that all those old VHS cassettes could be replaced by just six DVDs. Sounds too good to be true? It was - she lied. There are sixteen of the damned things winging their way to us.

Anyway, I must be going, the news is just about to start. I wonder what she'll be wearing tonight? Sorry, I mean I wonder how the Euro is faring against the pound and how the political situation in the Middle East is. I just hope she doesn't go for that off the shoulder purple number again.

Summer 2003

We won, well sort of !

For those of you who have been following our barn restoration project, we did it. We completed the project, as far as we could, and moved into the first phase of the project by the end of May.

All of our French neighbours and visiting experts had told me that it was not physically possible and I think, with the benefit of hindsight, that they were probably right. If they hadn't kept telling me that I couldn't do it, I probably wouldn't have succeeded.

The only fly in the moving-into-a-new-home ointment was the glaring lack of plumbing and electricity. Sue was somewhat shocked at the idea of moving in to a house without a toilet, flushing or otherwise and no lights. I explained that the lack of lights meant that she wouldn't be able to see the lack of a toilet. This did not go down well. The French plumbers and electricians belonged to the "he'll never do it" camp. But all credit to them they rallied round and connected up emergency services for us on the moving in day.

Things have progressed since moving in: We no longer have to flush the toilets with a bucket and the number of dangerous extension leads has gone down dramatically. In fact, we are now so much at home that we have welcomed our first guests to our new home. Sue's brother and his heavily pregnant wife have descended upon us for a long weekend. The lack of kitchen facilities has meant that we have had to eat out nearly every night - what a hardship - and I have had to take a whole weekend off from work to help entertain them. Yet another hardship! We all went out to the Aveyron gorge for a canoeing trip at the weekend - four hours of paddling along the cool river in 40 degree temperatures with plenty of stops for picnicking and swimming amidst the dramatic limestone tree-lined cliffs. It was hellish, but we survived. I even managed to capsize my canoe going over the last set of rapids to a rapturous round of applause. If somebody has to look stupid, why is it always me?

The high temperatures have necessitated the purchase of a plunge pool to cool off in, a must in the searing temperatures that we have been experiencing. True to form, Milly the mischievous kitten climbed up the side of the pool to drink the water within one hour of it being inflated and punctured it. She had to be chastised with a water pistol, but this has not deterred her one little bit!

We inflate it every time we get in and it looks lovely, just to the right of the rubble heap, next to the scrap iron, by the pile of old cardboard and not far from the gypsy caravan. To think that Sue's brother complained that the place looked nothing like the brochure - he obviously doesn't recognize a rural idyll when he sees one.

Courgettes and Caravans

I am not much of an expert on things horticultural, but I am almost certain that harvest time has come to the Tarn in the last week of June. I have come to this conclusion because every time I see another soul, be they known or unknown to me, they give me a courgette. All these people must either have been pessimistic about how many would survive, or optimistic about how many they would eat. I now have a hugely impressive courgette collection ranging from the standard supermarket issue to a few whoppers that have crossed the boundary to marrowdom. In fact, they may be marrows, or is a marrow a different thing? Anyway, as you can tell they have become a major thing for me. I really do need to get out more.

Other clues that harvest time is here are the Leviathan type combines clogging the narrow lanes. We watched the huge machine arrive in our hamlet while we were having sundowners on Friday evening. He got straight to work on the surrounding fields and he didn't stop once all night. I hope there was more than one driver, because he didn't stop all the next day as well, before leaving us as abruptly as he had arrived. A month or so ago an old friend from the UK called Phil came out here to work with me and live in a caravan in my garden with his wife and dog. We went to work as normal on Wednesday, cheese sandwiches and tea as usual, discussed upcoming contracts and went to look at a large new project for the autumn. All seemed rosy until Wednesday evening when they announced that they had had enough of France and were moving to Holland. After picking our jaws up off the floor we managed to ask "When?" "Not tomorrow - we have to pack the caravan up. The day after."

True to their word, by Friday lunchtime they were gone. This has left me in a bit of a hole as I have taken on a number of two-handed contracts, but I am sure that I shall manage. I even managed to wish him luck through gritted teeth. Apparently his wife disliked France and everything French - not the best starting point for a life in France. There are always casualties among the people who move out here. Life is not always what people expect it to be.

The good news is that our friend Helen has rescued a baby kestrel that her son has usefully named Falcon. Falcon the kestrel fell onto their balcony and was unable to fly as it still had its downy feathers and seemed to be abandoned. It wouldn't feed - until, amidst much derision and cries of "it'll never work" Les took all of his son's play-doh and fashioned a bird's head. He then put a pair of tweezers in the beak and tried to feed the bird some meat. It worked, and Falcon is thriving. Helen has borrowed a toy mouse from our cats and is going to train it to fly using a gauntlet. I'm sure you have seen the film. I am wondering if kestrels eat courgettes because I have a small surplus.

Sights and Sounds

I took myself out for a walk last night. It was hot and airless, I had eaten too much, the Professionals DVD was not grabbing my attention and I needed a spot of fresh air. I wandered to the top of a nearby hill to watch the sun go down. The hill belongs to a French neighbour and has a small derelict barn on the top. It is saved from English buyers by the fact that the electric and water companies won't run services to it. I sat and looked for miles across the rolling countryside towards the Gresigne forest and I couldn't help thinking 'this idyllic countryside is all very well, but there is way too much noise going on.' It was about ten in the evening and there was a combine harvester chattering away in the distance. When he gave up I could really hear all the crickets, cicadas and frogs yelling at each other. It appears that as soon as one chimes up, all the others join in and then have to shout louder to get themselves heard.

The sounds of these are nothing compared to the birds. There are a couple of families of swallows in the derelict part of the barn next door to us and their fledglings have just flown the nest today. They are flying around the barn in crazy circles, dive bombing Milly the cat as she tries to stalk them, flying into the house and creating a cacophony of sound. The sound of the birds is then drowned out by the lowing (I'm not sure what this means but if it means mooing in a disorderly fashion then it is the word for me) of cattle. How this comes to be, I don't know because there does not appear to be a living cow within five miles of us.

As if all of this was not enough to bear, the countryside is an absolute picture. The vines are a lush green and pushing out grapes, there are fields of sunflowers that seem to pop up overnight everywhere you turn, and bales of freshly cut hay in every other field. It is enough to make you want to build a motorway straight through the middle of it all and bulldoze all those oak trees with their oxygen-giving leaves.

The only thing that I don't understand is that if the countryside around here is so full of wonderful things, how come our garden is thick with every weed known to man? It is full of things that look like potato plants that have grown to about three feet tall in a couple of weeks and plenty of scary looking things that only David Bellamy would recognize. Very soon we are going to need a compass to get from one side to the other.

I suppose one solution would be to cut it all down - but that would be interfering.

Wheels

Hindsight is a wonderful thing. I am now wishing that I had spent, at some time, every spare penny I ever had on shares in Lycra. I had no idea how popular it was as a clothing item until the Tour de France came our way. The Tour de France arrived on Friday. In the days leading up to it, Lycra proliferated. Youngsters on their father's bikes and old men that really should know better could be seen pounding the lanes in the latest designer cycling gear. It seems that it is not enough to just watch the sport, you have to wear the gear and ride the bike in order to assimilate yourself into the once-a year event.

The great day arrived. I sagged off work early, throwing my tools into the van at lunchtime and explaining to the clients that I just had to go and see it. We headed on down to Cahuzac (pronounced Cowzak), a small town about five miles away that the race was passing through. Weaving around the 'road closed' sign, we drove up to the edge of town and abandoned the car along the road as everybody else had done. The stage of the race that we were seeing was not a straightforward race but a time trial. The cyclists were leaving at two minute intervals, starting at mid-morning and continuing into the afternoon.

The centre of the town was closed and busier than I had ever seen it. It was wall to wall Lycra and bicycles, it was more desperate than just a crime against fashion: I'm sure there must be a clause in The Geneva Convention about people with unsightly bulges wearing figure-hugging clothes. We swallowed our horror and threaded our way through the crowd, past the serried ranks of moustachioed, gun-toting gendarmes enjoying being paid to watch the cycling. (The single female gendarme had no moustache, but she did of course have a gun).

We settled down in a shady spot to watch the proceedings. As the gendarmes blew whistles, a police motorcycle appeared, closely followed by a helmeted Lycra-clad humanoid on a contraption that held few comparisons to the bicycles of my childhood - followed in turn by a support vehicle. Two minutes later the same thing happened again, except this guy must have been more famous because he also had a motorcycle film team and an extra car following him. The most popular rider had four vehicles, two motorbikes and a helicopter. Two minutes later... you guessed it, another bike etc. We settled down, bought a beer and baguette and watched a blur of metal every two minutes.

It was all free (you didn't have to pay for parking), well organised and great fun watching the huge caravan of people and equipment that follows these guys around the countryside. Also, if you were wondering where all the Americans and Australians have been this summer, they have been wobbling about the French countryside on bikes, wearing sunglasses, swigging from water bottles and trying to walk in cycling shoes. I think that I may actually be a convert to cycling. If we buy a TV aerial before next year I may watch the whole event, maybe buy a bike, but what would I wear?

It wasn't me

France is closing down. People are winding up their businesses left right and centre ready for the great August shut-down. We luckily managed to get hold of our errant plumber just before his holiday and held him in an arm lock until he had plumbed in our last sink and made the final connection for our shower. As soon as I let go he scuttled off into the sunset with vague promises of returning in September to finish what he had started. I shan't be holding my breath. We are still waiting for a telephone connection and a permanent electricity supply but have decided to write off the possibility of anything being done in August.

The festival season is still in full swing. Last night was the first night of the renowned Vaour festival - a week-long festival of clowns and comedy that takes place every year in the heart of the Gresigne forest. It was cool and laid back, with folk music, jugglers, acrobats, tables arranged about the market square under the shade trees, beer and wine to be sipped - and all for free. All of this subsidised by the arts bodies and the good old EU, or whatever that bunch of guys in Brussels represented by the blue flag with stars are called. If you want to know where your subscriptions end up, come on over to mainland Europe and see how they are spent. Thanks very much - we had a great time.

We went along to a party after the festival. It is not considered rude over here to turn up three hours too late and close to midnight - we were just asked to pull up a chair (after about twenty minutes of introductions and kissing of strangers). The only name that I managed to remember from them all was Trevor, and I knew that one already. True to form, I managed to get collared by the slightly drunk French woman that was unable to talk unless she had hold of a part of my body. We began pleasantly with small talk about how long we had been in France and her hand lightly grasping my wrist. When her hand moved onto my knee I began to worry; her grip tightened when she brought up the British invasion of Aquitaine and my kneecap was nearly crushed when she raised her voice and called me a killer.

I felt compelled to defend myself and protested my innocence - and was told in no uncertain terms that I was guilty as charged of the murder of Joan of Arc. What can you say? Accused of the murder of a semi-mythical figure from the dark ages who was probably half-mad anyway. I did try a defence; I took the Arc murder on the chin, but did say that it was William the Conqueror who started the whole invasion thing and that us Brits are just really Frenchmen trying to get back to their roots. Not the most popular argument with the French - or the Brits for that matter. We continued to spar into the early hours touching upon Napoleon, but we never did get to Agincourt. Maybe next time.

Help!

I had an emergency call-out the other evening. Our elderly neighbour, the octogenarian Monsieur Jollymar, came knocking on the door at seven in the evening asking for assistance to drill a hole.

Ever willing to please, I said 'of course' and asked what I needed to bring. He said that they had all the necessary tools and off we went. It turned out that in their high-ceilinged dining room they had a large ceiling fan with a wingspan of several feet that had come crashing to earth in the manner of Black Hawk Down. The mission, if I chose to accept it, was to scale a ladder, drill a hole through a beam, insert a bolt and re-hang the fan.

At this point I was surrounded by Monsieur Jollymar, his wife, her brother, his wife and another old lady probably hired in for the crowd scene. They had a combined age of well over 400 and were all stood there sweating, making clucking noises about the heat and looking dreamily upwards and remembering how wonderful it was to have a fan.

What could I say? 'Carry on sweating, one of you will expire soon and then there will be less body heat in the room? Of course not. I set to. The tools they offered me were elderly and not to be trusted, I went to fetch my own. The stepladder was a classic - a huge wooden affair that could be leant against a wall or opened out into steps. The first warning sign was the missing rungs. When I mentioned this I was told that they were designed for the mother-in-law. What really scared me was that the rope that held the two sides together was missing. Monsieur Jollymar stood beneath the ladder, gripped each side with his bony elderly arms and said that he would hold it for me. I had terrible mental images of me and the ladder collapsed on his head like a baby giraffe.

I went to fetch my own set of ladders, and in quarter of an hour a refreshing blast of cool air was wafting the room.

The next step was serious faces, rustling wallets and requests for how much they owed me. I explained that we were neighbours and it was just a friendly service. Delight and smiles and a bottle of Pastis appeared. So we sat down to an aperitif, the men at one end of the table and the women, all in their eighties giggling like teenagers at the other end of the table.

The conversation and Pastis went well, drifting from the Second World War to how we had settled in - until Madame Jollymar threw in the question of why didn't we have children. The concept of not necessarily wanting to have children does not exist around here, so I settled back on the old defence of it never having happened and a shrug of the shoulders. I was then told that I really must try harder and put in more effort.

I was then sent home, ladders on my back, with words of gratitude and encouragement ringing in my ears.

A Fete Worse than Death

I desperately need a holiday. Our local town, Castelnau de Montmiral, has been in fete for the last four days and it really is beginning to be all a bit too much.

The fete days seem to fit into a pattern; during the day there is generally something fairly dull and regional such as a honey market, everything grinds to a halt for the siesta and the evening meal and then kicks off again after ten o'clock.

Saturday night was rumoured to be the best night of all with the planned events being a meal of aligot and saucisse - aligot being a stringy cheese and mashed potato mix - followed by music and revelry.

We decided to pass up on the bangers and mash and go straight for the revelry. A friend of Sue's called Allison joined us for the evening as her husband had taken their kids to Avignon to visit relatives for the weekend.

Everything started well, a couple of drinks at home first of all to get us in the mood and then things started to go wrong. A much-needed storm blew up which forced us indoors and then blew our gazebo heavenwards before smashing it into a pile of twisted metal.

We decided to drive up to town in Allison's ageing Renault Five, which refused to start and then coughed and spluttered the whole way before finally asthmatically dying, fortuitously close to a parking space. I had to get out of the car and push it into its final resting place in the middle of a thunderstorm.

We made our way up over the ramparts of the medieval town like besieging knights of old and headed straight for the beer tent. The crowd of Frenchmen at the bar miraculously parted like the Red Sea in front of Moses for Sue and Allison and slammed shut behind them, leaving me literally out in the cold. I do exaggerate, the temperature was up in the 40s but it was raining and I was thirsty.

I finally managed to fight my way to the bar; Sue and Allison's needs were being taken care of and I felt the need to declare my dissatisfaction. I loudly proclaimed that I was really upset that I should turn up with two attractive females and that they should be stolen from me in a matter of minutes by a bunch of Frenchmen.

The Frenchmen stopped mid-banter, looked at me to see if I was joking or a trouble-maker, decided on the former and from that moment glasses of wine and beer kept appearing in front of me as manna from heaven.

The Frenchmen were pleased to have their Gallic pride massaged by the fact that they could steal an Englishman's women from him in less than 10 seconds, and the girls were perhaps just a little too flattered by the attentions of an 18-year-old rugby player.

I did try to regain my wards at several points but was soon put back in my place by a restraining glass of wine. I believe that the evening was great success but I did learn a very valuable lesson - never tell a female that she is old enough to be the mother of the man flirting with her; it hurts.

Grapes of Wrath

I had been labouring under the misapprehension that sunshine was a good thing. In fact, a really good thing - the kind of thing that we don't get enough of in the good old UK.

Around these parts, the farmers seem to have had too much of a good thing. They are not happy, not happy at all. We have had just three showers of rain since May. That combined with temperatures regularly in the forties, has dried the scenery to a crisp.

I would have thought that this was not all bad, because it means that you don't have to cut the grass very often, but apparently this means that the livestock don't have enough to eat. Let them eat cake, you may say - but the farmers around here have been letting them eat next winter's dinners, and this is not a good thing.

The local vignerons (wine growers) started the summer full of beans, happily explaining to me that the vine was a hardy plant that thrived on stressful conditions and would produce great wine from poor soil and just a few showers over the growing season.

It seems though, that there is stress and there is stress. And this summer has been serious stress. The sun has been ripening the grapes at breakneck speed while their toes have been bone dry and unable to send even a spoonful of moisture up to the berries.

There was a silver lining to this dark cloud, and that was that although there would not be so much wine this year, the wine that there was would be of a much higher quality.

Chatting to a vigneron friend of mine whose wall I was repointing, I made what I thought was a helpful suggestion: if the moisture content was down, why don't they just mix a bit of extra water with the crushed grapes and take it from there? It is only the same as watering the plants and it just cuts out the middleman.

You would have thought from the look on his face that I had just offered to defile his virgin daughter and murder the rest of his family. He explained that it was heresy to even suggest such a thing in wine country. Damn touchy, these wine types.

Just as they thought things could get no worse, and were harvesting three to six weeks early, the apocalypse arrived. I had just said to Sue that after a cool afternoon it looked set to be a nice evening when the black clouds came racing over and the wind picked up, reducing our already battered gazebo into its component parts. Lightening and thunder came followed by a hailstorm to end all hailstorms.

When they say hailstones like golf balls, they mean it here. The hail was so heavy that it smashed windows, cracked roof tiles and dented the roof and bonnet of our car - and the cars of everybody in the area without a garage. And of course it beat the hell out of any vines not already harvested, either stripping the leaves and grapes or bruising them so badly that they need to be harvested immediately before they rotted.

My top tip is to buy 2003 Gaillac, as it will be a rare vintage, but in the words of the song 'I must remember next time, to mix some water with the wine'.

Autumn 2003

A Bargain?

The days of picking up a French farmhouse with 10 acres of land and a breathtaking view for the price of a Ford Fiesta have well and truly gone in this part of the Tarn, so it was with some suspicion that I went to look at the bargain of the year; a whole house for £8,000!

The chap who wanted me to look at this once-in-a-lifetime opportunity was a Geordie called Dave whom I had got to know through a mutual acquaintance. He has just bought a bargain town house in a village near us and has got the scent for more bargains.

He is a structural engineer and specialises in oil platforms. He started his working life in construction and in common with most of us Brits has more money than sense - that is not to say that we have much money; just not very much sense.

When Dave called me up I was round there as fast as you could say 'cheap house' and eager to have a look. It was in the village along a narrow street where the other houses are being done up, stone-built, derelict and uninhabited for many years; so far so good.

We started to mooch around. It had a terraced garden, downstairs needed much work but had loads of great features, nice cut stones and huge solid beams. I was warming to the project. Sue had come with us and was starting to enthuse as well.

I could see a gleam in Dave's eye - if I was an estate agent, I would have known that he was hooked. We continued up and around the rickety staircases imagining the new layouts and cooing at the great features and then Dave showed us into the old sitting room. The room was not enormous but it contained the most humungous cut-stone fireplace that I have ever seen outside of a chateau. This thing was big enough to have a party inside and still have room for a chimneysweep. We all stood there awestruck. I could not believe that a house this size could support the weight of it - and how did they get it in?

I was sold, the place was a bargain until Sue asked us a question: 'Is that crack serious?' Dave and I looked at the wall to the left of the fireplace that Sue was looking at, at each other and then back to the wall. ' I didn't notice that and I'm supposed to be structural engineer' quipped Dave in his Geordie tones. And neither did I, and I'm supposed to be a builder, I muttered under my breath.

Further investigation revealed a rotten roof support that over time had allowed the full weight of the roof to push the flank wall out. Drastic measures required, a full roof demolition and rebuild plus a flank wall to be taken down and rebuilt, ouch!

We repaired to Dave's for a restorative beer and a discussion. After being initially crestfallen, a couple of drinks restored the glint in his eye and after throwing a few figures about he declared 'It is a lot of work, a lot of money - but it would be nice when it is done, wouldn't it?'

Heart over head; watch this space.

Muck & Bullets

Calling in the builders for many people is something like a second marriage, a triumph of hope over experience. Experience tells you that it is going to be noisy, messy, disruptive, expensive and that is only if they turn up when they say they will. Hope tells you that they will turn up, it won't be so bad and the work may even cost less than you anticipated.

My present client has just moved out of the hope part of the equation in our relationship. He had bought a house in a 'restored' state; unfortunately it had been restored by a German and therefore - apologies to any fugitive Germans in Dorset - done in dubious taste. In his Teutonic thoroughness he had all traces of stone and character covered in an extremely unpleasant crépis (render) that served to make the house as dark and sombre as possible. It is my contract to release the hidden glories of the stone beneath and let the house breathe again. This was all very exciting for the client at the planning stage - the first couple of days of crépis removal with a jackhammer exposing blocks of cut stone were awe-inspiring.

Unfortunately, dust creation does not stop at the initial demolition. Joints have to be raked out and then the best part of the operation comes in to play, the sandblaster. It is a moment of huge delight to a builder when you turn up on site towing a compressor behind the van, unroll miles of pressure hose, wheel out the sand hopper that looks like a mad Dalek, don the deep sea diver's helmet and, gun in hand say "Where shall we start?"

You can see every emotion fly across the client's face, "My God that looks expensive and powerful - is he really going to use that in my house?" and then despair and resignation sets in.

You can warn people about all these things but they only truly appreciate them when they are really happening and that is the time to just go ahead and get the job done.

Despite closing all doors and windows the fine sand from the external blasting found its way in through every small ventilation hole, but nothing was to prepare the client for the lounge wall being blasted. We carefully partitioned off an area of the lounge with plastic sheeting and I got to work. Within seconds visibility was down to a few inches and fine sand seeped through every pore of the house. The stone scrubbed up well but it certainly did leave a mess.

I found the client cowering in a corner, wondering how on earth we were going to clean the place up ready for when his wife got back from work; she is thankfully working away in Paris. After stowing the gear safely back in the van, a quick attack with a brush and a shovel soon sorted out most of the debris and pretty much left the inside as I had found it, except it was a little crunchier than before.

I happily drove off and left the client to recover himself before the next day's assault of sand and cement. I felt that I had repaid his hope in some ways; I turned up on time, the work was going to budget ... I was making a bit of a mess, but you can't make an omelette without breaking a couple of eggs, can you?.

All Geared Up

I turned up to do a small job for an English client in a nearby village the other day and was somewhat dismayed to find that I was unable to park outside the house to unload my tools.

In fact, I couldn't even see the house. The reason for this unfortunate turn of events was the renewal of the drains in this medieval village. In the UK the renewal of the drains would need to be discussed for ten years, put in front of a committee, protested about and then finally instigated on a three phase plan that allowed Mrs Miggins to hold her W.I. meeting on a Tuesday and made sure that the road would be reopened for pension collecting day.

Not so the French. When they decide to do something, they really go for it.

Imagine the scene. It is a tiny little stone-built village with barely enough room to swing a cat in the narrow alleys. In this area are two large Caterpillar-tracked machines that you would normally see working on a motorway, one large loading machine and several lorries. A few hundred thousand pounds' worth of gear, accompanied by no more than four workmen.

I've seen jobs in the UK, ten times the size of this piddling little engineering job, being carried out by half a dozen guys with picks and shovels and one ageing JCB if they were really lucky.

It reminded me strongly of a trip we made to Avignon a few years ago. It was a beautiful Sunday afternoon and the farmers, who were having one of their protests, had dropped lorryfulls of tomatoes in the street. The farmers were in fact having a lovely day out with their families, dressed in their Sunday best, having picnics and drinking wine in the sunshine. On the opposing side were the gendarmes, dressed from head to toe in riot gear: Kevlar vests, visors, Perspex shields, gas guns, dogs, riot vans. You name it, they had completely emptied the toy box and were ready to take on the Mongol hordes. A similar situation in the UK would have been dealt with by five Bobbies in their Dixon of Dock Green helmets and a bicycle for backup.

This is the basic difference between us. The Frenchman adores being kitted out and will not even think about taking on any kind of task unless he looks the part and has the gear.

We, on the other hand, take any kind of equipment display as a sign of weakness. Dig a hole with a spoon? Who needs a spoon?, I'll do it with my bare hands, I'm hard.

And that, my friends, I suggest is why the French finish work and then have the energy to party the night away while we slide off home to slump in a chair and fall asleep in front of the telly. Vive la différence.....

A Year in Pieces

This weekend, the lovely Sue and I shall be cracking open a bottle of barely-drinkable and celebrating our first year as asylum-seeking economic refugees.

It is times like this that you cast your mind back and consider what, if anything you have learnt in the last year. It is my privilege to share this knowledge with you. Here it is.

- Good friends are good friends, but crap business partners.
- The French only build new homes when their old one is full to the rafters with junk. They build a new bungalow next door and sell the old one to the Brits.
- French pop music is actually quite good.
- If you want to buy a pickaxe in France then the DIY store probably won't have one but you can get one in the supermarket where you will not be able to buy Paracetamol.
- You can do absolutely nothing for two hours at lunchtime, except eat.
- If you hate hot weather, festivals, drinking and generally having a great time then avoid France in August.
- Yes, French women are beautiful and sophisticated but rural French women do tend to resemble the livestock and on a hot summer's day, beware!

- Swimming pools are actually a necessity in fifty degrees of heat.
- Thermal underwear is a must have in winter and underwear needs to be stored in the fridge in summer.
- The average house contains a mind-boggling array of insects that often grow to the size of small mammals and are practically indestructible.
- People are really friendly and even the moronic plumber who never bothers pitching up is a really nice guy. People give you things, for free.
- The reason they don't sell English cheddar cheese is because it is too tasty and therefore constitutes unfair competition.
- The French state appears to be run for the benefit of the population.
- If you move abroad unhappily married then the chances are that you will remain just as unhappily married in a different place. The alternative chances are that you will rapidly become divorced or be madly swapping partners with other people in a similar position.
- You can buy houses for peanuts but you may be better off buying an old 2CV.
- Second-hand cars are dear, diesel is cheap, tools are dear, sand is cheap, deodorant is dear and wine is cheap.
- Therefore buy a new diesel that can carry a ton of sand, needs no tools to fix it, has air conditioning (no sweat) and can run on alcohol if needs be.

And the most important thing that we have learned is that we really quite like it here!

Hob Nobbing

I've had an epiphany, a Damascene moment. I have been to the mountaintop... the final segment of my circle of happiness has fallen into place.

All of the usual stuff is great: wonderful surroundings, business taking off, command of foreign language coming on, beautiful wife, blah, blah, blah but one thing has been missing.

I have, however, found the Holy Grail, King Solomon's mines, the lost city of Atlantis... yes, you have guessed it, the French equivalent of the chocolate Hob Nob.

It was a truly wonderful moment when I opened the packet of cereal BNs and discovered to my delectation a biscuit that is almost identical to its English cousin and transforms an afternoon cup of tea from a pleasant to a sublime experience.

Sue has not hesitated to label my enthusiasm as sad in the extreme, but I say that the French Hob Nob entirely fits my integration credentials: it fills a specific need but does not involve importing bits of England to France in that annoying ex-pat way.

Not much of a defence I know, but I did manage to make the packet last for two cups of tea.

On the business front, I have just finished the first demolition phase of a town house renovation, clearing out several centuries' worth of rotting farm implements, flaking plaster and about a ton of pigeon droppings.

Helping me in this endeavour is a neighbour of mine called Guillaume (pronounced Ghee-Yum) who runs a chambre d'hôtes and gîte business.

This is his quiet time of year and he enjoys coming along to lend a hand with those jobs which are just a bit too much for one pair of hands - such as lifting the 200kg antique oak beams that I had to install to hold up the ceiling after removing the kitchen wall.

And I have to say that he was a major player in the pigeon dropping removal operation, to the extent that he was cooing and preening himself on the way home.

We have had dramas on the pet front. Milly, our little French cat, badly damaged her paw by trying to climb where she shouldn't and had to spend the day at the vets. Our Belgian vet was very helpful and gave us back a sheepish cat who now walks on three paws and rattles with tablets, but will get better soon and no doubt will do it all over again. Learning from mistakes is not a common trait amongst felines.

My job next week is for my very first celebrity client, if you don't count the girl who cooked dinner for Chris Patten when he was down here.

It is to put up some partitions for the man who played Mark Darcy's father in the film Bridget Jones' diary. Apparently he got to say something about parking bikes at the end of the film and is also rather pleased to be getting another bunch of fees for making the sequel.

He may be a minor celebrity, but I suggest he doesn't know the secret of how to get a Hob Nob without flying all the way back to England.

What not to Wear

The flier looked harmless enough... a fashion show with arts and crafts, food and a charity auction. Ever keen to give anything a whirl and participate in local events, we headed off for a big Saturday night out in the local 'salle des fêtes'.

We were perhaps a little early arriving, and while we were waiting for the event to warm up it seemed rather churlish not to avail ourselves of the liquid refreshments being offered at scandalously low prices. The crowd was the standard mix - ruddy-faced locals and a slightly heavy smattering of ageing hippies and the knit-your-own-yoghurt brigade parading impressive varieties of facial hair.

After the obligatory aperitifs and five-course meal, the fashion parade began with a new age traveller type dressed in an electric blue catsuit. She was followed by a young guy in an extremely scary Ali G-style shell suit that seemed to have the potential to light up a small village with the static electricity coming off it.

At this point I had to collar one of the locals to find out what was going on. She patiently explained to me that there was a second-hand clothes shop in the village that is open one day a week and the event was to showcase what they had to sell. The shop sells every item for just two euros (about £1.40) and all revenue goes into the town and helps with keeping a library open and other useful causes.

Armed with this information, everything made sense, and I must say that the catwalk models did such a good job that we even tried to buy a couple of items - which had, unfortunately already been sold.

The crowning event of the evening was the charity auction of locally-made arts and crafts. At this point we were joined by a couple of French girls who were keen to try out their English, and we embarked on one of those ridiculous conversation evenings where questions in broken English are responded to by our equally poorly-phrased French replies.

The interests of communication would be much better served by each of us speaking in our mother tongue, but a lot of the fun would be lost. Sue explaining in French that because she doesn't work she sometimes gets bored at home. The girl replied 'Oh, you are very boring, then', it must have taken ten minutes to pull ourselves out of that one.

Sue started explaining about something high, or somebody tall, at exactly the moment when a particularly garishly painted long legged carved bird reached 20 euros in the auction - and she enacted a classic comedy moment by raising her arm to explain what she was saying. We were saved from ownership by the dubious taste of one of the locals, who saw the bird as a must-have for his house. We also missed out on the live chicken that smuggled himself in as a piece of living art.

I won't say that it was the craziest night of our lives, but as an alternative to a homemade jam festival it wasn't bad at all.

Winter 2003

Kissing Frogs

It has now been sorted. The accountant has been visited and the appropriate piece of paper has received its 'tampon' (this is the business stamp without which providence is unproved in France).

The bank has been approached to approve a loan and we are finally at liberty to seriously search for a home for us and the four furry fiends. We have launched ourselves into the 'frog kissing' part of the process with gay abandon, as they used to say in a more innocent time. I refer to it as frog-kissing because, as we all know and the lovely Sue will testify, you have to kiss an awful lot of frogs before you finally land yourself a true-life Prince Charming.

The frogs (or, more accurately, dogs) in the property market are houses that linger on the market for a variety of reasons - roads too close or too far, structural problems, flooding, factories too close, stone cladding, gnomes or any one of a 100 things that gives a pied à terre feet of clay.

We have just started visiting some of these properties and, as they are often advertised by several agents, you learn to make that all-important body swerve when you see a dog approaching. It was Saturday morning (rugby final day) we saw a restoration project that looked interesting and fixed up an appointment to see it in the afternoon.

When we arrived for the appointment the agent asked me to get my car so that I could drive him there. I agreed, and returned to pick him up. He opened the door, fell into the passenger seat and slurred a question at me: "Did you see the rugby?"

If the slur hadn't given it away the 50 per cent proof breath would have done. A herring could not have been more pickled. He proceeded to give me directions by slapping the windscreen at the last minute as we approached junctions, and shouting at other road users. We finally made it to the house, which had the look of a toothless crone who had not been loved since her early twenties: and as she was well over 80, that's not positive. As if this was not enough, the land had the appearance of Steptoe's yard, the neighbours had half a dozen sons with beat-up cars, many of the major walls had ominous cracks, and there was no more than a thin chain link fence separating us from the half-dozen slavering, howling hunting dogs that belonged to the neighbour.

Even though the agent pointed out that it did have a very pretty 'point de vue' and the bargain price was the equivalent of around £80,000, the answer had to be: no thanks old chum. We managed to cajole him back into the car, where he started to tell us how much it was going to rain that night with gurgling and gushing noises that were supposed to simulate rainfall. He finished this monologue by declaring "Of course, there is another possibility - maybe it won't rain at all!!"

This kept him laughing all the way back to the office, where we tipped him out onto the pavement. Send on those frogs.

Fogged off

I have news of good cheer to warm the cockles of your hearts over there in soggy old England.

You may be imagining us ex-pats down in the South of France, sipping gin and tonics by the pool, picking oranges off the trees and lazing about in hammocks. I am dismayed to report that nothing could be further from the truth.

The standard November fog has set in. That means that the only way you can find your way home (if you should be so foolish as to leave the fireside) is by leaving a trail of Hansel and Gretel breadcrumbs behind you.

This is extremely effective if you use a day-old baguette, as the hard-wearing nature of the breadcrumbs means that it leaves a Braille-type trail for the car tyres to follow.

When the fog eventually clears to the point that you can see the neighbour that you have been conversing with, it is in fact possible to see the rain that has been drumming on your head.

Believe me, when it rains down here it really does rain. None of that wishy-washy drizzly stuff - it's real fill-up-your-wellies downpours that can wash away small children and large houses that aren't tied down properly.

The rain is only part of the story. It is also becoming bitterly cold. The errant plumber not finishing the heating system has exacerbated this situation.

His deadline for finishing by the end of May has been postponed and missed so many times that I have lost count. The latest news is that it will be up and running by the end of next week.....

In the meantime, Sue appears to have been stolen and replaced by somebody with a size 22 body and a woollen face with two slits for eyes.

It was only when I opened the wardrobe door and found it empty that I realised she hadn't left me without saying goodbye - she was simply wearing everything that she owned.

The local farmers (the same ones that were tutting about the ferocious summer heat) are now shaking their heads and saying that it is going to be a terrible winter because it was a hot summer.

These are the same people who told me last year that the minus 12 temperatures in January were unheard of and would never happen again.

What is it about farmers? Do they have a special operation at childbirth that prevents them from saying anything remotely cheerful or positive about the weather? Some of these guys could give the British Rail 'leaves on the line' announcers a run for their money: too hot for grapes, too cold for grapes, too wet for grapes, too dry.....

It is not all bad news. Freezing cold weather means burst pipes, burst pipes means flood damage and flood damage means you need to call in a builder.

One man's misfortune....

Le Big Screen

Down here in the deepest and darkest corner of south-west France, it is quite easy to lose track of current affairs, trends and even people. In fact, I have only just been informed that Christmas is coming soon. It may have come already; maybe I need to get out more.

We actually have been making an attempt to get out more: we have been to our local cinema. When I describe the cinema as local, I mean it is a good half-hour drive through the forest - uphill, down dale (or gorge to be precise) and through a couple of time zones to the mediaeval town of St Antonin.

Those of you who saw the film Charlotte Gray with Cate Blanchett as a jolly-hockey-sticks type spy would recognise the town. That is to say, that you would recognize it in the summer time. It nestles at the bottom of the gorge in the shade of stupendous limestone cliffs, and does suffer from a lack of light and an excess of moisture during the winter months. In fact, the humidity there is about 100 per cent, to the extent that moss starts to form on exposed body parts if you stand still for too long.

What drew us to the town was the impressive multiplex cinema. I exaggerate. The word might be uniplex, perhaps. Ok, just a uni. The cinema is really what we used to lovingly refer to as a fleapit. It is a leap back to simpler times, and thankfully the only refreshments on sale are in the smoky bar on the other side of the street.

The owner awaits his customers eagerly at the door. His wife takes the money in the kiosk and lets her pony tailed husband show you to your seat. After illuminating the aisle with a torch and suggesting the best seat to you, he then disappears off to go and set the projector up.

There are no adverts for the Taj Mahal on the high street. They do, however, show current films of all nationalities and in particular, British and American ones in the version originale: that is to say, in the original tongue with subtitles in French. This is good, because although my French is not too bad I do struggle to understand a whole film, and the whole cinema experience does lose a little in the translation.

The other great thing about the subtitles is that you can learn an awful lot of argot, or slang. The film we went to see was the latest offering from Richard Curtis - called Love Actually - and there was plenty of scope for that.

It was the kind of film that makes you smile all the way through until you leave the cinema and gruffly mumble that it was ok for a sentimental load of old tosh. The experience was greatly helped by the absence of mobile phones, sweet wrappers, Coke or accursed popcorn. 21st century entertainment in a 20th century setting: what more could you ask?

Tea with Everything

I drove past our local Huit A Huit (8 'til 8) shop the other morning as they were opening their doors on the dot of 8.30. They will undoubtedly close at mid-day for two-and-a-quarter hours before finally closing at 7.30.

These are the things that I love about France; the stubborn, even bloody-minded refusal to conform to the international norm. This is also seen in their adoption and bastardisation of English words.

They plunder the English language with vigour and then stubbornly misuse the words that they have stolen. I bought a packet of crisps that were described imaginatively as Curlys, and those damned reconstituted, corn puff snack, monosodium glutamated items were as straight as arrows - they would not have curled if you soaked them for a month and then showed them a scary film.

It is a proven, well-documented fact that the French are set in their ways and steadfastly refuse to change in any way - so I believed when Guillaume came to work with me.

Things started off fine - I made a special effort to provide him with coffee at work. I'm afraid that I still can't learn to enjoy coffee; I drink it if I have to, but still prefer a nice cup of tea.

In the morning, we would stop at the boulangerie so Guillaume could buy a fresh baguette to have with his picnic lunch of cold meats, cheese, wine etc. We would stop for a suitably long lunch break, and so on.

I thought that I was gradually learning the French way of doing things until one day Guillaume asked me why I didn't make him tea as well. I explained that it was on account of his Frenchness and that he wouldn't drink tea. He pointed out my misapprehension and requested a cup of tea. I made him a cup of black tea and offered it to him.

'Where is the milk?' was the question that greeted me. I tried to explain that if you can get a Frenchman to drink a cup of Rosie Lee he certainly won't have milk in it. Wrong again.

Things started to get worse when my offer to stop at the boulangerie was refused in the morning. At lunchtime, all was revealed when he opened his sandwich box to reveal a full set of triangular cut sandwiches a L' Anglais.

Worse was to follow when he started eating quicker and requesting that we go back to work after just a half an hour for lunch. Before I knew what was happening, Guillaume had adapted all my long ingrained working practices, refused to start work without a cup of tea in the morning and was itching to go home at five o'clock.

When I took him to task about his lack of patriotic fervour he defended himself by saying that he was completely fed up with sitting around bored for two hours at lunchtime and not getting home before seven or eight in the evening. He liked the English system.

At least Guillaume doesn't speak any English, except for the fact that he did say 'hello' when he got in the van this morning. That is it - if he enlarges his vocabulary any more I am going to have to find a true Frenchman with a moustache, stripy shirt, onions and a bike.

Coasting

In true perverse fashion, we have just come back from a few days at the seaside.

We don't go to the beach in the middle of summer when the sea is warm and the acres of soft sand embrace you. We choose the middle of winter when the wind howls in from the Atlantic like a deranged Banshee and the sands are flying through the air and polishing your teeth.

This is a truly wonderful time to visit the Côte Sauvage: the West Coast of France that curves along the Bay of Biscay between Bordeaux and Spain. This area of pine forests and huge beaches is very popular with the French and other Europeans but not so popular with the Brits for some reason. It is our favourite destination for a spot of R'n'R. This time of year, the resorts are sparsely populated by a few die-hard holidaymakers, and a skeleton staff of workers.

One of the great delights of holidaying out of season is the ease with which you can achieve the normally impossible, such as parking in the parking spaces directly outside a hotel and getting a room in the first hotel that you walk into. The other delight is that you can pick that expensive hotel that you wouldn't normally contemplate and be sure of a fair deal.

If you are even smarter you can probably get an even better deal by booking in advance. We choose the tactic of driving about all-day and flopping in the first place that looks friendly, less economic but more fun.

The major difference between French and English hotels is the price. The places we stayed at were around 45 Euros a night (about £30) for a room with a shower and a sea view. Not bad. The major problem that they have is one of aesthetics. Who was it that declared it to be acceptable to put garish wallpaper and carpet on the walls of a hotel room, and patterned carpet at that - not to mention the juxtaposition of turquoise sheets and tartan blankets?

The interiors of most hotel rooms seem to be an explosion of bad taste. Perhaps that is not fair.... they don't seem to have used any taste at all - even bad taste at least shows some kind of effort.

This is one of the major questions that bothers me as I lay awake at night contemplating the troubles of the world. The French have such style and taste in the micro and macro sense: in the micro the Metropolitan French are beautifully coiffed and turned out in chic clothes (even the men) and in the macro their towns and cities are fabulously laid out (they gave the world boulevards and the Palace of Versailles). And yet in the middle they get things so completely wrong..... patterned wallpaper that continues across the ceiling is not acceptable and never will be.

I suppose it's fair to argue that when you have 15 foot waves breaking on an expanse of pristine white sand sparkling in the sunshine through the window, perhaps you don't need to bother about the décor. Did I mention the plumbing...?

Cannon and Ball

We have survived another one - the dreaded New Years' Eve bash has been and gone.

It has always been a bit of a strange event for me. For as long as I can remember, I have met people the next day who have told me about the fantastic time that they, had while I was silently contemplating the dullest evening of the year. Therefore it was with some trepidation that we accepted the invitation to a dinner party with our French neighbours and their 30 guests.

Sat next to our neighbours' prospective son-in-law, I had been given comprehensive instructions by his fiancée that he was terminally shy and that I was to try and draw him into conversation. I rose to the challenge, but one by one, my best conversational gambits fell by the wayside, mown down by monosyllabic responses. I was about to give up and either slit my own throat or his, when I managed to make a connection.

I got out of him that he worked for Aerospatiale and that he was working on the new super airliner that can carry the entire population of the Isle of Wight and still have room for a couple of tanks. This carried us for a while and as the wine flowed he loosened up a bit. We got on to the subject of the Second World War - not as bad as it seems, as we both shared a common interest in the history of warfare.

Unfortunately we both warmed to the subject to such an extent that our conversation was rapidly running beyond my vocabulary. I began to realise that I had dug a deep conversational hole for myself.

I was fortunately saved by the gifts being given out. (Everybody bought a two-Euro gift to put in the pot; these were accompanied by party hats and peashooters that fired paper balls at an alarming velocity.) Total war - a hell of a way to celebrate. I'm ashamed to say that I participated wholeheartedly and was soundly beaten by the French.

The meal was still going on - it must have run to about six or seven courses and uncountable bottles of wine of all different types. (The French eat all night and yet are nearly all as thin as whippets, drink all night and never seem to get drunk.)

The evening was rounded off by a choral cannon of Frère Jacques in which one group starts singing and doing the actions followed by the next, until the whole room is singing the same song but at different times. It sounds like a musical mess, but is in fact a great way to rouse a room.

We were the first to leave - much to the delight of the other guests, as they proceeded to make jokes about the English going to bed so early. We didn't take it too much to heart as it was about 3.30 in the morning.

Will we do it again next year? Only if I can sit next to somebody who wants to talk about something simple like nuclear fission or the plotting of the human genome.

Booked Up

People miss lots of things about the good old UK when they move away to far-distant shores, or even shores not so far away.

This can range from Marmite and crumpets to rain and fog. I know for a fact that Sue craves bizarre hair products that detangle, anti frizz, give extra body, do the vacuum cleaning etc. I have always been an addict to the written word. If it is printed, I will read it.

I'll read cornflake packets, instruction books for tools that I don't own, shopping lists. On one occasion I even read a Jeffrey Archer novel.

This addiction does have worrying effects. When I have a stack of books in front of me I am quite happy and relaxed, but as soon as I get to the last one in the stack I start to get nervous and restless, pace backwards and forwards, bite my nails, drink too much tea and generally become even more of a pain in the neck to the long-suffering Sue than usual.

This situation is usually best solved by a visit to another stranded English person. (I have already cleaned out the local bed and breakfast of all books left by their visitors.)

The victim needs to be well-researched, by probing questions about their background, schooling and interests. Computer nerds, sports freaks, hyper-intelligent people who understand what Stephen Hawking is going on about and the less hyper-intelligent that think Harry Potter is a good read for an adult are cast aside like last weeks' newspaper (that I also read cover to cover and back again.)

A cursory glance at the victims' bookshelf can sometimes be misleading. Many's the time that a victim has nearly been cast aside by the dubious taste of their spouse. The entire works of The Readers' Digest given prominence on the top shelf because they look tidy, may be hiding a rag-tag bunch of great books that could keep me going for a month.

My current victim is also my current client. He has bought the house I wrote about some time ago that is not much more than a pile of second-hand building materials in an approximate house shape. His current interest is getting me over to his place so that he can discuss the project, and this situation is made acceptable by his once-large library of books.

Every time that I visit him he opens a couple of bottles of beer, we step into the lounge, I field off a few questions, make my excuses and as a parting shot say "Is it ok if I borrow this?" - stuffing the book that I have had my eye on for the last 20 minutes under my arm and running out of the door.

The only question is whether or not his library can last to the end of the project. He could end up with an empty bookshelf and a half-finished house unless he starts importing some more books pretty damned quick.

Chainsaws and Grand Designs

The trickle of Brits leaving the homeland and seeking a place in the sun (although after three weeks of rain and drizzle this seems like a misnomer in this part of the world) is becoming a flood.

Barely a week seems to go by without meeting a couple of new fresh-faced Brits who have just bought a huge property with loads of potential. Having now been out here for over a year, we are entitled to look upon ourselves as old hands and to nod sagely and knowingly as we are told tales of woe about dealing with the electricity board and how difficult it is to heat an old house with doors and windows that don't fit and a roof like a colander that looked so adorable in August. The type of person who is emigrating to France seems to have changed in recent years. 10 years ago it was either retired people who were reaping the benefits of having worked for a company with an index-linked pension scheme, or hippies looking for an alternative lifestyle living off the land and the French benefit system.

The new émigrés are often in their 30s and 40s. Having just made a packet on selling their home in the volatile English housing market, they have been able to swap mid-terrace suburbia for their own plot of land with a huge pile of stone in the middle of it.

Almost without exception, the first thing that the male of the species does is to go out and buy a chainsaw. There seems to be many reasons for this. The first is that it is a great big toy that makes loads of noise, and the second is that it can make a huge difference to your surroundings.

In the unskilled hands of a novice, a chainsaw can cut a swathe through a 100-year-old orchard, leaving the proud owner with a denuded garden and a pile of firewood, which he can proudly contemplate while reflecting upon how impressively he has tidied the place up. A pile of logs looks great in January when you think of huddling around the fire, but come next August that rather diminished pile will be a reminder of how welcoming a few shady trees can be in searing temperatures.

The second characteristic of the house buyer is the need to do something with all the outbuildings, barns, sheds and kennels which organically grow alongside a house. The answer - for everybody - is to make it into a gîte or holiday home. This will provide an income later on, and in the meantime, a project for suburban man. Suburban man comes equipped with all the skills needed to renovate an old stone property: he has a drill and he has put up loads of shelves.

Most of these grand designs are destined to remain at pretty much the design stage. If they didn't, judging by the number of projects that I have been asked to look at, then the number of holiday properties waiting to be filled in France would accommodate the entire population of Western Europe. At the end of the day, a design is a dream and there is no harm in dreaming - so send us your chainsaw wielding masses. We can always replant the trees.

Making a Mark

Renovating old properties can often be a lot like being an archaeologist, poking around with dusty old fossils.... and that's just the clients.

Some of the things that you discover are pretty obvious and run-of-the-mill, such as blocked-up windows that were hidden to save on taxes. Some things tell us a bit about the times when they were done. The most common find is old newspapers - copies of La Dépêche going back to the beginning of the last century. The discovery of these old bits of rolled-up newspaper wedged in to cracks tells us that builders back then were just as lazy as they are today, and were happy to try and get away with using rubbish rather than mixing up or cutting the correct materials.

Digging up concrete floors can yield up all kinds of weird and wonderful reinforcing materials. I have come across old deckchairs and even a lawnmower - much cheaper than reinforced steel.

Working on old agricultural buildings has made me certain that when I am king of the world the very first thing I am going to do is to pass a law banning the use of concrete by farmers. For one thing, they put the damned stuff everywhere. Secondly, when they put it down they usually make it at least two feet deep, and this is not a lot of fun for those who come along later and have to remove it.

Sometimes the work carried out tells us more about the fashions of the time than the people doing the work.

I am often called in to remove crépis (render) from the outside of stone buildings. In the last century it was obviously considered to be only the poor who lived in stone houses, so people spent their money on paying plasterers to cover their beautiful local stone buildings in anonymous crépis. It is incredibly satisfying to break off the layers of cement, sandblasting the stone back to life and repointing with lime mortar mix to restore the original beauty of stone.

The fashions of the 1960s and 70s deemed wood in the house as old-fashioned and led to houses being stripped of internal oak beams (which could well have lasted for several more centuries) and staircases that were wonky but serviceable. These were brutally replaced by fake marble staircases and poured concrete floors, accessorised with liberal lashings of Formica and PVC furniture. The owners at the time must have felt as if they had well and truly arrived. I have lost count of the number of times I have been asked what people can do to restore lost character. The first thing to do is to look in the outbuildings, because there is one thing that the rural French won't do, and that is throw anything away. It is not unusual to find some of those old beams and replace them strategically to soften the effect of the concrete.

It does make me wonder what future generations of builders will be asked to do to my renovation work. Maybe that rendered finish could be the next big thing, and what with retro chic... well, perhaps we'll keep that Formica wrapped up nicely in the barn.

Sleeping on the Job (Unpublished)

The latest mission in the dangerous and exciting life of two builders in the South West of France was to track down and purchase a whole bunch of railway sleepers for a couple of landscaping projects.

Calls were made and brains were picked until we finally found an address for a marshalling yard in the backend of beyond. We duly set out with vans and trailers in-tow and tracked down the yard.

We found the office with the obligatory surly SNCF petty official sat in front of his steam powered computer screen. After ignoring us for ten minutes he finally deigned to acknowledge our presence. Guillaume did the talking and we were sent into the yard to help ourselves and told to pay for them when we had enough.

Suffice to say that shifting diesel soaked eight foot long lumps of solid oak is not the easiest job in the world and by the third trip we had had just about enough of it.

We were just loading the last couple of sleepers on to the trailer when an official looking railwayman came ambling over with his hands in his pockets. He started off making small talk, enquiring about what we were going to do with them and chatting about railways. He seemed a little nervous and finally plucked up the courage to hesitantly ask us a question, did we really need a Facture (bill or receipt)? He then started to explain how that with all the lengthy paperwork the price of each sleeper comes to at least 7 Euros each (less than a fiver). Sensing an angle Guillaume enquired if he would be interested in a cash payment. His ears pricked up, his eyes brightened and he suddenly became hugely animated, even offering to help us load up.

Deciding that shady deals were no place for a foreigner I left them to it. Finally, on the way back I asked Guillaume how much we had paid for them, he said "I managed to get him down to five Euros." "That's good. At five Euros each for three trips of sixteen at a time."

At this point Guillaume had to point out to me that although we seemed to have made three trips by physically going to the yard three times, we had only really made two trips and so he had just paid for thirty two of them.

I was scandalised and mortified. Surely this counts as a robbery, we could be arrested. Guillaume gave it his best Gallic shrug and explained that the SNCF was nobody and was therefore incapable of being robbed. He also pointed out that the railway official was not going to declare his little windfall and would probably go out to the nearest bar with his work colleagues and have a damned fine night out. In this way we would be helping out with the welfare of the brave railway workers, raising morale and helping the railway system to run efficiently and on time.

We had done a good thing, but if I do get called to account for doing good things can somebody please send me one of those cakes with a file baked inside it?

Les Visiteurs

Two fortuitous events occurred last week. The first was the final cessation of six weeks of torrential rain that turned babbling brooks into raging torrents and small ponds into navigable lakes. This was succeeded by a front of warm weather that had us wearing T-shirts and dining al fresco.

The second and complementary event was the arrival of visitors from the land of our birth: Sue's brother, his wife and their new baby popped down to see us for a few days.

With the return flight for all three of them from Southampton at just a 100 quid, it seemed rude for them not to take advantage. And talking of advantage, they ate us out of house and home and drank everything that they could find in a bottle including my aftershave.

At this stage, I do have to admit that they didn't arrive empty-handed. They were well primed. The news of visitors is like a red rag to a bull for us exiles scraping a living in the barren expanse of rural France.

It is true that a lot of English products can be bought over here. Our local Intermarche has a small English section which sells Heinz Baked beans at 1.50 euros (£1) a tin and PG Tips for the price of a small caravan. You can buy Twinings tea off the shelf, but it is blended for the French palette - which is to say, not very impressively.

The major thing that we miss being able to get are vegetarian products. A vegetarian product in France is about as useful and welcome as pork sausage at a Jewish wedding, and has about the same number of takers.

Vegetarianism does exist in France. It does not exist, though, as a moral issue for lovers of fluffy bunnies, but only for the type of nutter who goes in for colonic irrigation followed by self-flagellation with a birch branch and an ice-cold bath. If it moves and can be caught, the French will eat it. Fair play to them, but it doesn't provide much of a market for meat substitute items.

It was with great glee that Sue whizzed off an e-mail to her brother with a wish list, and we eagerly awaited their arrival. The great day came, and we picked all of them and their huge suitcase up from the airport.

Sue and I noted the impressive scale of the baggage and nodded at each other. Obviously we had a suspicion that they might just have a fair bit of stuff on account of the baby, but we had high hopes and couldn't drive home fast enough.

We got them in through the door, popped a bottle and pushed them in to their room with hints such as "You'll be wanting to unpack that great big heavy bag."

I'm pleased to report that they didn't disappoint. We now have quality tea bags aplenty and a freezer full of genetically modified soya protein pretend food that will keep us going for months.

On top of that, the baby hardly cried at all, the sun shone and they were great company. But unfortunately Sue's brother is still telling jokes. Every silver lining...

Starving in Eden
(Shrugging off one's responsibilities)

In the feast and famine world of construction that we inhabit, there has been precious little feasting going on of late.

In fact, we have even had to ask the church mice that inhabit the barn next door if they could spare us a morsel of cheese. They just shrugged and suggested we eat wiring looms, like they have to. Things were taking on a somewhat grim complexion. Several contracts had all come to an end at the same time and the horizon was looking as empty as Saddam Hussein's social diary.

Guillaume was luckily having a couple of weeks' holiday. As he left he looked at me in a rather sad and forlorn way and asked if I thought there would be any work for him when he got back. I shrugged and said "maybe".

I'm really warming to this French shrugging stuff - it kind of divorces the shrugger of all responsibility for what they might have just said. I sat down that night and looked at all the dévis that I had recently prepared and sent off and contemplated the horrible prospect of having to ring round and start begging for some of the jobs. Not my style - I prefer it if they come to me. I was on the verge of contemplating trying a bit of despairing.

It is true that I can be a bit laid-back. I usually never really worry about not having any work lined up. Something always turns up. I tried to worry myself, however, by imagining what was the worst that could happen to us if nothing came in. I'd have to sell my soul and a couple of the cats. Sue might have to go back out on the streets, but that would still only give us a couple of euros.

It wasn't working, I was still not worried. Then the phone rang. On the other end of the line was an English guy by the name of Gilles. His real name is apparently something like Malcolm, but he changed his name by deed poll to Gilles in honour of his motor racing hero Gilles Villeneuve.

He had spoken to me about a town house renovation a year ago and the project seemed to have fizzled out and died a death. The good news was that it was alive again and he wanted me to do the work. Hurrah, hurrah! Stop burning the furniture, we can afford a lump of coal.

All was going swimmingly - I met the architect, we sorted out some costings and I was just getting the job teed up ready for a start on Monday when Gilles called me up to go for a meeting. I turned up at the meeting, fully prepared for a 'dear John' sort of message, when he dumped three more projects in my lap, all to be completed by June. Who said that it was just buses that come along all at once?

Spring 2004

Cupboard Love

Ever in search of a bargain, we have begun to search through the many junk shop superstores that inhabit the environs of all major French cities. These emporiums to all that is gash operate as a bizarre hybrid between a pawnshop and a flea market, and they are often found in modern prefabricated tin sheds sandwiched between DIY and furniture stores.

The idea behind these shops is that Joe or Jean public takes unwanted items into the shop and tells the shop how much they want to sell them for. The shop displays and sells the items, taking a commission on each sale.

This does lead to some bizarre pricing. An ancient computer keyboard may be on sale for 50 euros (£30) when it actually has no value whatsoever. There is, of course, an interesting flip side.

Sue's huge clothing collection was getting a little tight for space, so we went in search of a wardrobe and looked among the furniture selection in a particular favourite of ours, which goes by the catchy title of OK Cash.

We were exposed to an Aladdin's cave of exotic delights. They had electric blue sofas, Formica-covered corner bars with banks of lights that would make even Del Boy wince, and coffee tables perched upon dolphin's noses - and that was just the better items. But if you do not allow yourself to be sidetracked, there are some pearls.

The item that took our eye was a solid oak Breton wardrobe with fabulous carving and an intact mirror on the door. I realised how solidly made it was when I tried sliding the door off its hinge to see if the thing would dismantle. As the door slid up, its full weight nearly tipped me off balance and into a stack of crockery.

A quick inspection proved it to be well-made, solid and demountable and all for the bargain price of 180 Euros (£120) - I am no expert, but I am sure that you would have to pay several times as much for it in the UK.

I can only really put this down to the fact that the majority of the French are at a different point in the cycle to the Brits.

We threw out all of our hand-crafted wooden items in favour of Formica and chipboard tat way back in the 1960's and 70's. This is what is now happening all across France, if the queues outside IKEA are anything to go by. So, the price of old quality items is not far off rock bottom. Give it another 10 or 20 years of handles and drawer fronts falling off, and people will be mad for a bit of lasting strength. Unfortunately, this new discovery has led me to a new-found fascination with wardrobes. I have just seen a superb art deco item with matching bed that is an absolute steal.

The only problem is that we don't need any more clothes-hanging space. Perhaps I could take Sue clothes shopping?

On second thoughts, some prices are just too high.

Long Tom Kitten

We once again find ourselves playing host to yet another temporary visitor, but this one is of the four-legged variety.

I say four-legged, but although he has three good legs, the other one is largely made up of 500 Euros (£350.00 plus change) of titanium plates and bolts.

He is a ginger tom kitten who sustained his injuries either by jumping off a high ledge, being sat on by a toddler or from his best playmate who happens to be a 10-stone Rottweiler.

Either way, his injuries are such that they prejudiced his chances of going skiing in the Alps with his owners and thus he has fallen into our care for the week.

This was fine by me until I realised the full implications of having another body in the house. I had become quite comfortable with my present situation in the pecking order - at number five, below the existing cats.

I was not prepared to have my lowly place in Sue's affections so cruelly taken by a ginger tripod (triped?) with a penchant for trying to climb anything higher than a grasshopper and licking noses. The two options open to me are either to strangle the cute fluffy bundle of mischief or to wait the week out and try to recover my position before anything else comes along. It may be wise to choose the latter.

On the work front, jobs have come in aplenty. We are about to start work on three bed and breakfast rooms and a restaurant in the middle of the historic medieval city of Cordes sur Ciel (Cordes on the sky), a striking city which appears to perch impossibly above the swirling morning mists. Very romantic to look at but hugely impractical to work in, as the original builders with their horses and carts would no doubt have been able to confirm if they hadn't all succumbed to overwork and the plague.

The good news is that we have got the work. The bad news is that all the work has to be done before the tourist season or the end of June at the latest. That gives us all of four months to do at least six months' worth of work.

The restaurant provides the greatest challenge as it is at present no more than a derelict shell. It is literally no more than four walls, and two of those are not in very good shape.

It will certainly be a test - a blank canvas, and all that.

In order to help Guillaume and I rise to the challenge we are taking on a French plumber by the name of Patrice. He is married to an English girl and spent many years living in Croydon and therefore speaks faultless English in a South London way. (I think they call this an oxymoron, like 'military intelligence').

We are itching to get cracking with the project and start to win some time back. If only it was possible to train a small ginger tabby to find his way around a French wiring system.

Digging for Victory

It was with mixed emotions that the titanium-legged atomic kitten was handed back to his rightful owners after his week long sojourn with us. It was good to no longer hear his pathetic whining when he was sent back to his cage after his 10-minute exercise break, but it was sad to no longer see him chasing away our other cats who outweighed him by about three stone.

Sue begrudgingly gave him back, muttering something about nobody else being able to look after him as she could. I was just looking forward to a good night's sleep.

Sleep has been very welcome this last week because we have started full bore into the restaurant renovation project for an English couple. They bought a derelict building next door to their house with the aims of turning it into a restaurant, and when they received the keys to the building they discovered that it had a barrel-vaulted cave built into the hillside at the rear of the building.

It was my dubious honour last week to clear out the cave and see exactly how it could be incorporated into the restaurant. It was a little like Howard Carter and Lord Carnarvon breaking into the tomb of King Tut, except there was no sand, just damp - and the most valuable antiquity residing next to the rotten bed that fell apart in my hands was an empty beer bottle circa 1970.

Undeterred, we set to digging out half a metre of stinking damp soil in order to create a floor fit to eat off, or at least fit to put a table on without it sinking to the bowels of the earth.

The sun has apparently been shining, but Guillaume and I have been blissfully unaware of this fact as we have toiled away with pick and shovel in middle earth. In fact, we are beginning to understand why moles don't bother with eyesight down there; there isn't a wonderful lot to see.

The only thing that helps me to keep my slender grip on sanity is listening to our local radio station M Energy. It is such a cheap affair that they don't even have a DJ, they have about 15 CDs and 10 jingles which are just set to random play.

This might be a bit much for a normal mortal to take but it is great for me, most of the tunes are 15 years out of date (perfect) and I get to learn all the lyrics (even the French ones), which means that I can sing my little heart out all day.

I thought we were having a lovely time until Guillaume could take it no longer and declared that he was on the verge of suicide. I asked him what the matter was; was it the hard digging, the damp conditions, the darkness, global warming? He shook his head in response to all my questions.

Apparently the single worst thing in his life is my singing. Ungrateful swine, you do your best to make the world a brighter place and what sort of gratitude do you get?

Tourettes de France

If you have ever read or seen anything about renovation projects at home or abroad, you will be familiar with the difficulties involved in finding a skilled tradesman.

They are either incompetent or not available for the next five years. So it was therefore with some trepidation that we called the electrician to carry out his first fix on my current project, my regular electrician being indisposed. With great surprise we discovered that he was available to start the next day.

He came as a recommendation from my colleague Guillaume, who had used him before and warned me that he was a great electrician but a bit mad. No problem, I said, and engaged his services.

Bernard the electrician turned up on time - a good start - and shook hands. When I say shook hands, I really mean that he enveloped my hand in a huge paw that would have been outsize on a lesser man but this man was truly enormous, a great bear of a man.

He seemed gentle enough and we established that he wouldn't be able to get in the loft space, so we decided that we could do those bits for him. I did notice one odd thing about him; his arm looked a little ragged, I just put this down to a skin condition.

Everything went well with the first room that he wired, all the points put in nicely and level, all his mess cleared up. We had truly chanced upon the Holy Grail, the perfect tradesman. Why had Guillaume called him mad?

The second room was a different kettle of fish. The first room had been lined with placo plâtre (plaster board), meaning that all the wiring could be pushed through the loft and behind the walls, but in the second room it was necessary to cut channels in the concrete floor. This would have been okay if the concrete had not been so hard and the electrician not so averse to dust. He began to get angry, very angry, and in fact he voiced his anger about us not using placo plâtre by punching the wall and screaming 'Placo, Placo!' several times before returning to his disc cutter. He would cut a little further and then collapse in screams of 'Placo'.

He then charged past me, ran outside and started butting his head against the stone wall. He returned to his cutter and started punctuating his work by biting his arm, really biting it hard. This explained his ragged arm.

Unable to intervene in any way, I just left him to blow himself out. When we stopped for lunch he seemed to have calmed down until, he started telling me about his money worries.

Apparently he had poured all of his money into the family home and now that his mother was moving into a home, his brother and sister were throwing him out.

He then started blubbering like a baby. This huge guy was crying and wailing that it was so sad that he worked night and day and was going to end up destitute. We returned to work, he screamed, he bit himself even harder, he threw inanimate objects around the room but he completed the job without actually breaking anything.

What price perfection?

Keep off the Grass

Springtime is not only a time of unsurpassed joy and frivolity, it is also a time of great worry for anybody unfortunate enough to be the custodian of a garden bigger than a postage stamp.

Last time I looked at the small parcel of land that surrounds us it was an obedient mat of green weeds and grassy stuff that clung to the soil as neat as the day that I strimmed it to death a couple of months ago. I have just looked out of the window and been confronted by a fecund vision of grasses reaching for the sky, a multicoloured vision of weed flowers and perhaps a small band of pygmies on their way to hunt wild boar.

I am considering taking a few lessons in French lawn care. They do not subscribe to the English love of perfect weed-free lawns; partly due to the fact that the weeds are practically bomb-proof and partly due to the advantage of keeping some of the green demons. If you kill off all the weeds at this time of year you will have a lovely lawn for one month or maybe two, but then when the Southern sun burns its way through you will be left as the proud custodian of a miniature version of the Oklahoma dustbowl. If you leave those weeds in place you will have greenery all year round.

The next lesson in French garden care, short of buying heavy duty machinery from Massey Ferguson, is to blast everything with herbicide. Over here they are not so squeamish about the use by private citizens of potentially lethal cocktails of chemical nastiness. If you have green where you don't want it, hit it with a spray. This takes less time than walking around with a strimmer, and if you use something sufficiently unpleasant you only have to do it once a year. Huge swathes of boundary fences and roadsides around the French countryside look like Vietnam after a visit from a B52 laden with Agent Orange.

This heavy-handed approach means that your average Frenchman can afford to be relaxed about his front garden. When his mate turns up to share a pastis on his way home he may well park his ageing, leaking Citroen or tractor squarely in the middle of the front garden. If the lawn has survived this far, a few tyre tracks and the odd puddle of fuel are not going to do any more damage. What would cause an apoplexy back in the UK will not welcome any more than a Gallic shrug.

Many a Frenchman can be spotted enjoying an evening drink as he watches his mad Anglais neighbour spinning around in circles on his sit-on lawn mower trying to tend to the six acres of lawn that he is desperately trying to keep down before trying to revive it in a few months time.

Watch and learn.

Gnome Worries

As we were driving home from work the other day an interesting story came on the local radio. This was remarkable in itself because the general fare on Gaillac's own M Energy radio station ranges from a 35 year-old tractor for sale with a full MOT to a cheese festival at your local village hall.

This story, picked up from the English press, told of an unemployed Englishman who had been making a career out of stealing cars and returning them to their owners after giving them a full valet. This absolutely creased up my colleague, Guillaume, who turned to me and declared that the English truly are insane.

Unable to defend our national honour upon this point, I decided to put a case for mitigating circumstances. In essence, my argument was the British love for mischievousness, or being just a little bit naughty. To illustrate this point, I started to tell him the story about an Englishman who had one of his garden gnomes stolen, only to receive a ransom note and a photo of his gnome in a far-flung corner of the globe. I don't remember the precise details but he received photos of his gnome at Ayres rock, alongside the Trevi fountain and so on, until it was eventually returned to his owner. A bit of harmless fun.

Guillaume listened to this story with mouth agape, obviously impressed by my skills as a raconteur. Describing what exactly constituted a garden gnome, with all the fishing rod actions and descriptions of red and white toadstools took some doing, I can tell you. Then I discovered that he knew all about them. He declared "Vous avez gnomes de jardins en Angleterre, aussi?", amazed that the British had embraced the Gallic pursuit of keeping small bearded men in the garden. The debate about which nation started this peculiar tradition is one that could go on for days or months, but I was interested to learn that in France, as in England, there are legions of gnome lovers, as well as legions of people dedicated to their eradication as an affront to taste.

In these days of the expanding kingdom of Europe and the Entente Cordiale, why keep trying to homologise our two nations by implementing more and more regulations? Just give people a simple form to fill out. Do you like little men in pointy hats in the garden, yes or no?

All the yes's could meet together and collaborate to make a gnome-filled Utopia. Language barriers would disappear and friendships would be forged upon a common ground, while their nemesis, meanwhile, just as enthusiastically plotted their downfall. Traditional nationalistic enmities would be forgotten and a brave new world would appear, English and French side by side in a common endeavour.

There is of course one major flaw in my plan. What happens when the two sides meet? There could be blood on the streets, civil war in suburbia. Perhaps we could ask the Germans to mediate? Or maybe we should just consign this idea to the great hands-across-the-Channel ideas bin, along with The Channel Tunnel, Concorde, The Common Agricultural Policy, the use of deodorants...

Les Invisibles

This week, I have mainly become invisible; or at least, it has seemed that way to me.

The reason for my feeling of diminishing visibility, my existence as a kind of Cheshire cat without the grin left behind, has been the necessity to visit French builders' merchants.

The project that I have been recently working on is to make three chambre d'hôtes (B&B rooms) with en-suite facilities. At the beginning stages, all is fine. Bags of cement, sheets of plasterboard etc are all held in stock. When you get to the finishing stages and need things such as tiles, bathroom suites, doors etc these all have to be ordered.

This does not really sound too complicated: make a phone call, the stuff arrives two days later, they deliver it and you whack it in. Not so fast readers - this is France.

In the first place, it is no good trying to place the order by phone. The message will be taken by somebody who is just marking time until the end of the day, and even if they do write it down they will just chuck it straight in the bin.

When you subsequently phone up to check on progress, you will be told that it is on its way. This will go on until you get mad and go down to the shop, discover that the order was never placed and that nobody apparently ever spoke to you and you have to start all over again.

Secondly, the concept of stock seems to have ceased to exist. I am told that this is due to the fact that, in the past, unscrupulous traders used to use any profits to buy stock at the end of the year in some kind of tax avoidance scam. In order to close this loophole, all stock is now classified as profit, nobody in their right mind wants to make a profit in France - therefore no stock.

A simple bathroom suite will take at least quinze jours to arrive. This translates literally as 15 days, but can mean anything ranging from a few days to the gestation period of an elephant. And if you want the stuff delivered, take out a mortgage - all delivery is extra, and a significant extra at that.

Delivery also brings in the added danger of your goods sitting ignored in a warehouse until somebody can be bothered to deliver them, usually in several pieces because they didn't have a bit of rope to secure them.

This is why, a few weeks ago, I was obliged to lose several days of my life being ignored in various plumbers' merchants and tile warehouses as I ordered the necessary goods. This has the added complication (and this is the fun bit) of being against the clock. Trying to order from more than two shops before the lunchtime shutdown is physically impossible. Hey presto, the whole day is lost. No wonder as an artisan you receive a 30 percent discount - you need at least that to pay for lost time.

Picking up the goods is even worse. Half of all of my orders all arrived this week, so I have been schlepping backwards and forwards, showing my receipts, being invisible to various warehouse staff, getting half of what I wanted, and guess what? I'll have to do it all again in quinze jours to pick up the rest.

A nice place to visit,
but you wouldn't want to live there.

I have just come back from a flying visit to the good old UK. This has prompted several questions, apart from what was the weather like. The biggest question is what has changed in the 18 months since I last set foot upon the shores of fair Albion.

Well, in short: small relatives have become bigger and older ones have become smaller.

There is now one car for every man, woman, child and pet in the UK and they all appear to be on the M27 outside Eastleigh airport.

Good friends are still good friends but inexplicably seem to have managed to carry on a successful life without us (of course, they might just have been putting on a front).

People in the UK have not grasped the continental way of shopping - that is, going in to a shop, looking around, wasting the shop assistant's time and then leaving empty-handed after deciding that it is all too expensive.

The UK is instead buzzing with people buying everything within sight before it all runs out.

After spending 18 months in darkest rural France, even the sleepy market town of Dorchester seems like a megalopolis of frightening modernity. There aren't even any chickens in the street. England appears to have become a rich, Jag-driving, golf-playing, flash uncle to the poorer Europeans who are following on their tractors.

In the supermarkets, the Brits appear to have out-Europeaned the Europeans with a more comprehensive range of pastries and coffees than it is possible to find in their true heartland.

Brits have become noticeably bigger. Teenagers are Goliath-like. The boys wear shoes the size of small boats and the girls are just busting out all over.

Pound for pound, the Brits are way ahead of the French and possibly even catching up with the Yanks. A pint of bitter is thankfully the same size that it always was and tastes just as good, but now requires a lot more cash to buy it.

The final question about my return visit to the land of milk and honey is; do I yearn to return to the adrenalin rush of spend, spend, earn, earn, never pay it all off?

Now I am sat back here in southern France, listening to the cicadas chirping, the cattle lowing and that annoying guy on his tractor in a far distant field, I have to say, I'll give it some thought.

But not too much.

Summer 2004

Spare us from the tourists de France

Summertime is here. It has hit us like a sledgehammer down here in the Tarn. The temperature has rocketed from a disappointing 10 or so degrees, up to the scorching 30's.

This has of course sent every able-bodied, man, woman and child (not to mention those other types that close-knit, inter-bred communities throw up periodically) scuttling for the nearest tractor with which to make hay while the sun shines.

The flip side to this idyllic rural scene can be seen in the tourist honey pots, which are beginning to stir in to life. As I try to make my way to the local builders' merchants I am assaulted by the sight of acres of bare white flesh, topped off by baseball caps - and believe me, this is not the kind of flesh that you want to see bared.

North America and Northern Europe are chiefly to blame. I am considering writing to customs in these countries and requesting that each person leaving should have their bags checked. Any ill-fitting T-shirts, shorts and sandals should be confiscated on the spot and the perpetrator should be supplied with a boiler suit and a hearing aid (the hearing aid in order that they can hear the van which is two feet away from them as they meander along the centre of the road).

No matter what time of the year, there is always one constant - one thing that can be depended upon, never changing, guaranteed. I am of course referring to the retired chap in the builders' merchants. Amazingly, this is one phenomenon that completely transcends racial and cultural barriers. When you screech in to the builders' merchants, desperate for 10 sacks of cement in order to finish the paving around the hanging gardens of Babylon, he is there.

He is habitually dressed in autumnal nylon and often with those annoying glasses that he either has to remove or look over the top of. He will normally have at least two members of staff fully occupied in attempting to supply him with either one piece of wood, or an obscure piece of plumbing, which was last employed on the engines in The Ark.

You stand behind the elderly gent, fuming and wondering why he isn't in the special homes that they have for people like him. (They call them B&Q in the UK or Brico Depot over here.)

When he has finally finished haggling for his discount, he will pay with his pennies or centimes from his little purse.

At this point, I feel myself close to bursting and decide I will leave empty-handed before I commit a capital offence. Well, I would leave if that damn car with the Caravan Club sticker was not parked in the way.

Organic Growth

If you haven't got any money then the best place to go shopping is at a market. If you are in France then go to a French market - they are supposed to be famous for them.

Fitting comfortably into the former category and indubitably into the latter, we decided to take ourselves off to the local market on the bank holiday weekend. This was not just any old common or garden market, this was a genuine Bio market (pronounced in French as B.O. always guaranteed a snigger from the Brits). This means that everything for sale was 100 percent organic. When I say everything, I mean everything, from jam to sheep's wool loft insulation and clothes made from plants looking suspiciously like cannabis.

It was really quite interesting to see exactly how unappetising organic growers can make things look. People were selling things like carrot pâté that had the pallor of a 10-day-old dead goldfish and pancakes that looked more like pans than cakes.

It does make you rewind to remembering why additives and fake colours were invented in the first place - they were designed to make things look appetising and good to eat. Surely getting rid of them is like trying to uninvent the wheel?

The most striking thing for me about the market was the people, they were all stylish and chic - that is, if your idea of 'stylish and chic' is matted dreadlocks and a preponderance of primary colours matched with assorted piercings.

I have to admit that for people following the organic life, with no unpleasant chemicals allowed in to their bodies, they looked like possibly the unhealthiest specimens that I have ever seen.

I was feeling an overwhelming urge to pour a can of fizzy tartrazine-laden orange juice down somebody's throat to see if it might bring some colour back to them when Sue pointed out another anomaly. They were almost all, without exception, smoking heavily - not in itself unusual for France, smoking is still considered to be a vital part of a balanced diet - but this was a much higher than average percentage.

The only reasons for this seemed to be a natural urge to redress the health balance, or sheer desperation from having to live on a diet that would make an ascetic monk chuck his habit on a bonfire, buy a motorbike and join the Hell's Angels.

In fairness, I do have to say that some of the display stands selling solar heating panels and ways of capturing geo-thermal energy from the bowels of the earth and using it to boil a kettle were really starting to capture my interest. In fact, I even got as far as buying some stuff - I bought myself a couple of tomato plants.

Not being a great gardener, I was not exactly sure what I was buying, but I did know that I like tomatoes and the stallholder looked like Ben Gunn, so I decided to go for it. On arriving back home, I worked out that I needed to plant the them green side up, and each time I look at my little organic plants settling in to their new life, I can't help wondering if they wouldn't be happier with just a couple of drops of chemical fertilizer.

Where there's a Villa

The great Trev and Sue house search has just reached a new level of intensity. In fact 'intensity' is probably a little too mild, as we are about to become SDFs (sans domicle fixe): that is to say homeless.

Our route to SDFdom was simple: the house that we have been living in rent-free for the last year thanks to the generosity of our friends has been sold from under us.

Our situation has been rather ambivalent; we have been trying to help our friends sell the place, showing people around and dealing with estate agents, trying to present the place in the best possible way.

On one hand we have been wanting to help our friends successfully sell, and at the best price. On the other hand we were rather hoping that nobody would want to buy it, thus keeping a roof over our heads. It is done now though; the deal has been signed and we have less than three months to get our act together (as we should have done some time ago).

Sue has been trawling the Internet and short-listing properties, which I look at when I get home from work. I find it difficult to focus after a hard day, and Sue has taken to interposing the list of houses between me and the fridge holding the ice-cold beer. Carrot and stick, builder and beer.

The criteria for a new home represented pretty standard fare for the Brit in search of a new life in La Belle France: an old farmhouse built of stone with a sun-drenched terrace, vines crawling over the pergola and views across the rolling fields. Our quest has taken us to heaps of tumbling stone in godforsaken flyblown dumps. Well, that was the ones within our budget. Others were more in the pop star price band. The South West of France is no longer a secret. It is now recognised as so stunningly beautiful that even the French want to live here, and prices reflect that.

Our search finally led us to a modern villa perched on the side of a fabulous gorge. It has a swimming pool and no major works to be done! Let's just go back and check that wish list: old property, bags of character, to be restored... no ticks in any of those boxes. We looked over the hideous neo-Grecian pine-clad monstrosity with the estate agent, being careful not to go near the garage that contained a host of slavering wild dogs.

Sue and I looked at each other and recognized what was happening - we had actually fallen for a modern breeze block pile. It was like admitting that you enjoy a visit to McDonalds or prefer the Rolf Harris version of Stairway to Heaven. We liked a villa!

Well, that's not entirely accurate. The house was junk, actually, but the view was, as they say, to die for. They wanted an arm and a leg for it. We have offered an arm and a small part of a leg and are waiting for the response.

If we don't succeed, desperate times and all that... anybody interested in a kidney, one careful owner?

Forging Ahead

The current restoration project is now beginning to take shape - it is a small town house set in the mediaeval lanes of Cordes-sur-Ciel that has to be taken from a state of utter dereliction into a state fit for a tourist. This has necessitated a complete internal demolition, sandblast and re-jig, and there is nothing a builder enjoys more than creating dust, debris and mayhem. This has, of course, brought to light a few problems that are inherent in old uninhabited buildings. The building has settled down on its haunches and looks a little like a pregnant woman who has eaten one bag of chips too many - there is a huge bulge around the midriff and consolidation is necessary.

This involves getting hold of some long tie rods, some decorative cross pieces and tying the building back together before its waters break all over the street and bury a herd of unsuspecting tourists beneath a sea of freedom-seeking stone.

So I dutifully set off to the local ferronier (blacksmith or foundry) to order the necessary items. I went into the workshop which was full of sparks, black dust and the deafening din of metal being hit very hard and waited to be acknowledged.

I was somewhat surprised when the patron looked up from the workbench, lifted his brazing mask and was in fact a woman. Don't get me wrong, I'm all in favour of women doing jobs that have traditionally belonged to men - as Sue will testify as she sits in front of the telly drinking cans of beer and asking where her tea is - but I was somewhat surprised to see it in Cordes.

France has still a very masculine culture. Men sit around, drink wine and play boules, while the women make preserves, gossip and basically do everything that needs doing for little or no recognition. The countryside is very conservative and women are generally kept in their place. However, there is one possible route for female emancipation. Businesses are not often created in France, they are more traditionally handed on to the offspring.

When the father dies and the offspring is not especially male, then this provides the female with an opportunity.

This appeared to be the case with the ferroniste, who is more than capable of holding her own in a steel debate. Something similar has also happened at the builders' merchants - you can't get a much more masculine environment than a merchants, but the principal one in Cordes is watched over by the steely eye of Madame Gautier.

She sits in her office, high above the hustle and dust of the yard, with her patterned housecoat on, keeping track of every cement bag and nail that leaves her yard. Apparently her husband died young and left her with a family and a business to support. Unable to leave it to her young son, she rolled up her sleeves and got on with it, and in her spare time makes a fair fist of her second job as deputy mayoress of the town.

It is comforting to realise that in this brave new female-dominated world there will still be place for men - somebody has to drink the wine and keep the boules court in use. Vive la révolution !

Taking the Plunge

Down here in the sunny South West of France (turn left after the last cow at the back of beyond), where temperatures are getting close to 40 degrees, you need to choose your friends with care.

By this, I am not implying that the heat turns normally mild-mannered librarian types into axe-wielding psychopaths, although it probably does. In fact, it definitely does, Sue has just screamed at me for not being able to use the computer properly. In her defence, I would have to admit that my PC illiteracy could probably stand up in court on a justifiable homicide charge - and that is also not to say that she is a librarian type. Help!

What I was really getting at is the need to choose friends with an integrated body cooling system, also known as a swimming pool. What you may consider to be a luxury item is in fact a necessity when you have been deep-fried on a building site or lost ten pints of body fluids cleaning holiday gîtes.

Sue and I, finding ourselves victims of these respective hostile environments, sought solace with our good friends and neighbours Guillaume and Catherine, who run their chambres d'hôtes holiday complex across the next field from us. Playing host to an inexhaustible stream of Northern Europeans seeking the sun means that they have to maintain a well-kept pool, ideal for bringing down that body temperature by a couple of degrees.

Unfortunately, as they are good friends, a quick swim can lead to an aperitif and then to another, then to a meal, and before you know it, a lost evening - or maybe a found one.

Before you could say 'who are those strange people in our swimming pool?', we found ourselves sat at the large dining table helping G&C play host to a collection of red-skinned tourists who were making short work of the wine stock.

One of the guests was Belgian; I spoke to him in French and he replied in English. I did wonder if we should be less polite and use our own languages, but I was more interested in what he had to say. He informed the table that Johnny Hallyday is in fact a Belgian.

In order to give this statement the gravitas that it deserves, I had better explain who the hell he is. Johnny Hallyday can variously be described as the French Cliff Richard (he has been going as long and has his roots in rock'n'roll) or the French Tom Jones (women of a certain age swoon at the mention of his name, and the rest of humankind wonder why).

He is known as Le Rocker, his face has been lifted so many times that he shaves his forehead and he bears the Gallic scars of way too much wine, women and song. He is constantly in the papers for paternity suits and divorces. He is, in short, a model Frenchman, except that he is not - he is a Belgian. Whoever told me there was no such thing as a famous Belgian? Shattered illusions. Next they'll be telling me that the Pope is a Pole. I need a swim.

Guess Horse coming to Dinner

Last Friday evening was one of those balmy summers evenings that seems to last for ever.

It had been another hard week at the French rock face and we were enjoying a spot of recuperation with our friends and neighbours. We sat outside enjoying the stored heat of the day, sharing a meal and just a few drops of the local grape juice. It would be hard to describe Gaillac wine as the best in the world, but it seems somehow disloyal to drink anything else.

The evening was going extremely well; the debate had ranged from films to the death penalty: I even managed to get past that one without once again being accused of killing Joan of Arc. The peace was suddenly shattered by a fierce scraping and crunching of gravel. I am employing a little artistic licence when I use the word 'peace': the racket at night is deafening, with crickets, cicadas, frogs and combine harvesters all competing to make the loudest possible noise.

Guillaume was duly dispatched to investigate. I took advantage of his absence to top up my glass of Armagnac and receive a kick on my shins from Sue. No gain without a little pain. Guillaume came back around the corner with a big grin on his face and proudly announced that he had found a horse on the terrace.

We all laughed politely and then asked what was really on the terrace. He insisted that there really was a horse on the terrace - not a big one, but a small one. We went to see and yes, there was a foal standing on the terrace, looking as if it was in its natural habitat.

This did of course prompt a few questions, such as what the hell were we supposed to do with it? This was partly answered by a whinnying from afar: it was the rest of the family group calling for their lost member. The cries simply served to excite the foal, which started jumping and thrashing about as we tried to shoo it down off the terrace towards its mother without falling on the headlong descent down a very steep slope - no mean feat for a bunch of half-cut diners in the blackness of a French night in rough terrain.

With persistence and a little luck we sent the young fellow on his way and found the cause of his breakout: the electric fencing had been knocked over. We established that there was no current going through it by attaching Guillaume to the wire and watching his hair; it stayed flat on his head. We repaired the fence and returned to continue our meal as if nothing had happened.

Unable to let the matter rest, I felt obliged to insist that a horse turning up just before the Tiramisu was not a normal occurrence. Catherine countered that a horse turning up was nothing - the other week, she had come downstairs to prepare the breakfasts and found a sheep stood in the middle of her dining room.

You just can't compete with that!

Les Boys

I had a call from Patrice, my erstwhile plumber, a couple of nights ago. His wife is an estate agent and she had found us a cheap townhouse to buy and renovate.

How cheap? That was my first question and when I received the reply, 15,000 Euros (ten grand in sterling) I was somewhat sceptical.

I have seen houses for these kind of prices before and there is usually a damned good reason for the cheapness. Ever willing to take a punt, however, we fixed up a time to go and meet the vendor and view the ruin.

We met up and went off to see what was what, Pat told me a little about the vendor: he was an entertainer and was selling up because he was off on a world tour. I was prepared for an arty or Bohemian type. Nothing prepared us for the sight that greeted us when Colin opened the door. The beige stilettos were the first thing that I noticed, followed by American tan tights, up to a suede cowgirl outfit complete with tassels all the way up to a long blonde wig and make-up that had to have been applied by a short sighted plasterer.

What can you say? What do you do in the middle of the day in a small village in rural France when a cross-dressing Englishman called Colin answers the door? Do you kiss, shake hands, what? I shook hands with him and said 'Alright mate?'.

'Yeah, not too bad.' was the answer. 'You come to look at the ruin? Here's the keys, help yourselves.' We took the keys, walked out of the door and looked at each other as if to say, 'Did you just see what I saw?'

Unfortunately the answer was yes, we did just see either an extremely unattractive woman or a strangely-dressed gentleman. We went and checked out the ruin next door. It was righteously deserving of the term ruin - in fact, the castle on the top of the hill that was laid waste by the English in the 1700s was in a better state.

The view of the river was nice and there was a very strong possibility that the river would be even closer in the winter: you would probably be able to do a spot of fishing from the stairs leading to the ground floor.

After nearly falling through rotten floorboards, seeing the sky through the roof and choking on the smell of damp that was rising, falling and meeting in the middle we decided that maybe this wasn't the project that was going to make us millionaires. We gave the keys back to our mate Colin and we were just left with one lingering question: Had we interrupted something, was he rehearsing an act, or had he got up like that for our benefit?

I think I know which theory I'm going with; I saw the look he gave Patrice, I'm sure that there was just a hint of electricity in the air.

Before you know it Pat will be turning up for work in a frock and singing Judy Garland numbers. Who said buying houses was a drag?

Can't stand the heat?..

It is now the first week in August, the mercury is showing 40 degrees in the shade, every self-respecting French artisan has packed away his tools and cleared off on holiday for the month.

This leaves just one Englishman, several mad dogs or cats and a trusty sidekick providing the sole artisanal output in the whole of the Tarn region, if not France.

As usual, I have chosen my August project with care, forward thinking and common sense. Last year it was a loft conversion with restricted head height. That was like being inside a Tandoori oven with a mad mullah beating you on the head with an oak beam every five minutes. This year I have surpassed myself. I am converting an open-ended barn into two holiday gîtes. This has involved digging footings in rock-hard earth and pouring a concrete floor in blast furnace conditions. Now that the temperatures are just reaching their peaks and the sun is as fierce as it could be, I am outside block laying. I am currently working 20ft in the air on top of scaffolding that is hot enough to fry œufs on, building a gable end out of pleasantly light coloured concrete blocks that are gradually blinding me the higher I get with them.

I am not really one to complain, but I will anyway. It is damned hot, in fact it is so hot that we have had had to start work an hour and a half earlier in order to benefit from the early freshness.

At home the cats are unhappy about the fur coats that they have been issued with - they are trying to rectify this injustice by spreadeagling themselves out on the floor tiles and trying to draw all the coolness out of the subsoil. Sue now refuses to do anything that involves wearing more clothes than a bikini. This is fine when blagging free use of a swimming pool from friends, but can be a bit tricky when visiting the bank manager about our mortgage.

We seem to have got our French mortgage sorted. I've jumped through hoops and presented certificates that I didn't even know that I had. Did the bikini help? Probably not, because the bank manager is a woman, but then you never know.

Our new house to be has a swimming pool, and it is our determined ambition to be in there by the end of August. This could be rather a pipe dream, as to succeed with this will require the co-operation of French bank people and solicitors and we all know where they are in August.

None the less, we remain undaunted. It is this spirit, which keeps me climbing up on to that red-hot scaffolding and laying blocks. It is this spirit, which made us win at Agincourt, and look at the benefits we have reaped from it.

The losers are currently all sitting on a beach somewhere sipping cool drinks and relaxing. To the victors, the damned gable end. That's history.

Do you know who I am?

Some things in life never cease to amaze, such as why the 2CV was ever deemed to be an acceptable form of transport and why Brits abroad still remain convinced that speaking their own language louder will make Johnny foreigner understand them.

I was amazed yet again when I went in to my local insurance office. It was a simple visit in order to renew my motor insurance, they had asked me to bring in my driving licence so that they could make a copy. I walked into the office, only the second time in my life that I had been in there and before I even had a chance to say 'bonjour' in my best Dorset French the woman behind the counter said "Bonjour, Monsieur Morris" (pronounced Maurice) tapped my name into the computer, put her hand out for my driving licence and knew exactly why I was there.

This kind of hyper (no, that's not strong enough, mega) efficiency is so far way ahead of the cutting edge of our information highway-obsessed world that it is in fact nearly old-fashioned. It seems that in France, knowing the name of a client, what they do for a living, how many pets they own and their preferred flavour of ice cream is considered to be important.

In shops that I only frequent occasionally, such as ones that sell anything that costs me money, I am greeted as a long-lost son and am in mortal fear of a fatted calf being slaughtered and the seven-toed daughter being offered to me in marriage.

I have to say that this is all rather alien to me - I spent years with the same bank in the UK, I used to go in and pay my cheque in every week, nobody ever acknowledged that I had ever been in before or even that I existed. In an odd way I was quite comfortable with the anonymity, but the down side always comes when you need a little help.

I have just been sorting out a French mortgage for our new house and the young lady who has been processing my application has been painfully efficient. She shines like a Rolls Royce Spirit of Ecstasy mascot on a World War 1 battle tank - she is bright and eager, but the machine behind her is lumbering, unwieldy and slow.

This is reflected in her face when she pushes yet another sheaf of papers in front of us to sign, initial and approve. She looks at us as if to say: "I know it is ridiculous that you have to sign each one of these 40,000 pages, if I could change it I would, but I can't." To her credit, she has sorted out a mortgage in quick time and she even knows who I am when I telephone.

In fact, I was so enthused by the helpfulness of everybody that I have recently come across, that I didn't even flinch when my first French income tax bill arrived on Saturday.

I looked at the number, smiled, wrote a cheque and posted it, there and then, glad to be paying for a system where I am more than a number.

I pay, therefore I am.

Chaps and Thongs

August..... and the fete season is back with a vengeance.

Not for us guess-the-weight-of-the-cake and knobbly knees competitions. In France, the annual, entertainment filled, all eating and dancing, fete, is held by the community for the benefit of the community.

The first element for Homo Anglais to grasp is the fact that none of the proceedings appear to begin before 10 o'clock in the evening. This goes sharply against the grain, as we are ready to party before seven, but generally getting ready to collapse by the time that the French are revving up.

The second element is partaking of a meal as part of the evening as a social occasion. Surely a meal is either taken as a stomach liner before the event or a coup de grâce afterwards, such as a curry or a kebab? The alcohol is yet another matter - the price of a glass of beer or anything else is set at one euro fifty (about one pound) and at that price you can fill your boots. However, look around the tables and there is hardly a French man or woman with a glass in front of them. Restraint is practised to an alarming degree; no drunkenness, no fistfights and no vomiting. We are well beyond the southerly limits of the Viking influence.

Our local fete up at the bastide town of Castelnau de Montmiral seemed to start well on Friday night. There was moules frîtes for the foodies and plenty of cheap wine. The music started to rev up, it was getting close to 11 by this time (yes, the 11 just before midnight) and things were just starting to happen. Then some dancers came on stage and it became obvious that the event organiser had either had a head fit or had got his wires seriously crossed.

Our local town is really very local, rural. Yokel, interbred, charming.... call it what you will, it is in the middle of the country, there is no crime and a scandal is somebody not marrying their next of kin. On the stage was what can only be described as exotic dancers. There was an oiled-up half naked male dancer with a Peter Andre six-pack who had obviously never ploughed a field, accompanied by two scantily-clad females who didn't look as if they had ever pickled a gherkin. Jaws dropped, false teeth and straws hit the deck as the trio gyrated to old disco numbers. At least the outdated music helped remind me where I was.

The final blow was to come when they had a break for a costume change. The girls came back on stage, prancing to Shania Twain wearing an extremely loose interpretation of a cowgirl outfit. (This consisted of not much more than a pair of chaps and a G string). Standing in the middle of rural back of beyond with this floor show reminded me strongly of the scene in Apocalypse Now when the playboy bunnies put on their show in the Vietnam jungle. Strange days...

Autumn 2004

Well, strike me

I'm sure that you don't need me to tell you all about freak weather conditions. We have even been sent pictures of the new canal/highway in Boscastle.

We may not quite be able to compete with that particular apocalyptic flood, although Sue was rather unhappy to note that the temperature dropped below 30 the other day and I did see a wispy cloud just last week.

Our particular weather freak is the thunderstorm. We are not far from the Pyrenees and therefore we do get to see plenty of them when those weather fronts come in from the Atlantic. We have become used to them, but last night was exceptional.

As I was turning off the lights I looked up at the sky and was greeted by the type of sight normally reserved for John Simpson when he visits Baghdad. There were bursts of bright lights and forks of lightning with more tines than you could count. The kind of sight, which crosses from scary to fascinating... unfortunately, an aerial display of that magnitude comes at a price.

Sue received a call from a friend this morning, asking for help with a clear up operation. Our friend lives in a large house on an exposed hilltop; she has the highest building around and has no trees around her. I'm sure that you can guess the rest: her house was struck big-time.

One of the first sights to greet Sue when she surveyed the devastation was cat food all over the ceiling. The lightning struck the chimney, travelled down the metal flue liner and blew the chimneybreast apart, ripping up the floorboards from the first floor on its way. It smashed through the wood-burning stove, entered the floor tiles, travelled across the floor and exited beneath the cat bowl, blowing the floor tiles to smithereens and sprayed what was left of the ceiling with cat food. Our friend was fortunately not in the kitchen area, which bore the brunt of the blast, but was in the lounge. This was better, but not entirely safe: the electricity surged through the house along the wiring and leaped out of a socket to give her a nasty blast to the leg. Every cloud has a silver lining, and all this drama gave her a damned good excuse, as a lone female in distress, to call out the Pompiers, who promptly arrived wearing full kit, including those space age chrome helmets.

They seemed to spend a little longer than was absolutely necessary making sure that everything was safe and filling her with horror stories about other strikes that they had seen. The conclusion was that if she had been in the kitchen, she would have gone the same way as the cat food. Quite a sobering thought.

It turns out that when she bought the property she had considered getting a lightning conductor fitted. A female's practical thinking; I would have just looked at the lovely view and not considered the danger.

She was dissuaded, though, because the all-knowing locals told her that the church spire was higher so there was already a conductor nearby. Lesson to be learnt - never listen to those who know best, unless you want a visit from the Pompiers. Now there's a dilemma for you, girls.

Breaking Dreams

I am feeling really bad today. In fact, I am feeling worse than that. If Scrooge were alive today and today was Christmas day, I would be Scrooge but just a bit meaner.

The reason for my fall from grace lies with a young couple who are madly searching for a property to buy in our area. We got to know them because they came to look at the house we are living in as part of their search; we gave them a cup of tea and gradually became friends.

Their search has been hastened by rapid approach of a new family; the girl is on her last visit before she is deemed unfit to fly, or deemed too fat to get into an aeroplane or whatever criteria they use to stop people giving birth mid-flight.

During our many chats over a beer it has become obvious that I am a builder by trade and it was in this capacity that I was called out to go and survey the house of their dreams. I say 'house of their dreams' because only in their dreams could the gaping hole of a building that had not been inhabited, except for mice, for at least 30 years be called anything approaching a house.

It suffered from all the worst elements of French farmhouses that are for sale for renovation: namely it was too damned big, there were too many rooms, too much roof, too many outbuildings and just too much building to renovate.

It was like going to visit somebody who had just given birth to a two-headed monster and having to say something nice such as "At least you'll be able to have two different hairstyles."

What can you say? "You are completely mad - throw your money off the nearest bridge and save yourself a whole bunch of heartache?" I was struggling for anything positive to say. Some of the beams were quite nice, but all the rotten wood in between detracted from the charm somewhat. I looked at the couple: they were lost in dreamland, they could see all the little children running around the playroom and all the happy holidaymakers in their guest rooms.

This was the killer: not only were they wanting to buy a heap of junk like so many before them, they were planning to convert the tumble down tractor shed into holiday gîtes. Planet France calling the UK: please stop sending over dolly daydreamers who imagine that a life in corporate finance qualifies them to restore derelict buildings and run leisure complexes.

A heavy dose of reality was what was needed. I told them the facts. I gave them a guide to renovation costs, told them how much the roof was going to cost them and then asked how much was asked for the derelict shell.

You could have knocked me down with a feather. The owner wanted a cool 280,000 Euros (nearly £200,000). In my estimation, it was worth half of that, at best. We added up the renovation costs with the purchase price and came up with a figure that should buy you a small island somewhere.

They took all of this on board, looked away from the wreck towards the rolling hills and remarked what a lovely view it was. A lost cause...

The Trench Connection

Have you ever considered digging a trench down the middle of a medieval cobbled street, or perhaps beating yourself across the back of the head with a blunt and heavy instrument while inserting hot needles beneath your fingernails?

Whichever option you choose, the results are likely to be largely the same. Fate has sent me such a task in the archaic town of Cordes - it was presented to me as a tumbling wreck that had not been lived in since God was a boy.

It had probably been a happy family home in the days when a cow on the ground floor was seen as central heating and an efficient sewerage system was a window close to the location of the chamber pot. It is this last matter which is vexing me - the house has never been connected to any services - electricity, water or waste - and due to the fickle nature of modern man it needs all three.

The first part of the puzzle was to visit the Mairie and make a tentative enquiry - this yielded a small result. We were sent two goons with a truck and a sewer map, which might as well have been written in Albanian.

Tweedle Dumb and Tweedle Dumber looked at the map, paced the street, turned the map upside down, rolled some cigarettes, scratched their heads and declared that there were no sewers nearby.

At this point, I feel duty bound to tell you that we were stood in the middle of a hillside town. Knowing that you are never more than three feet away from a rat at any time, and I have seen a good few of them in this town, I felt that I had to intervene.

Having recently connected into a sewer pipe in this town that appears on no council map, I resorted to a method that the brothers Grimm had not considered - I opened my eyes and looked around and, sure enough, down a few steps was the telltale roundness of a pipe. I pointed this out, much to their consternation. They got the hump, got back in their truck and called for backup.

This took the shape of Monsieur Coufignal, the minister of works, who turned up sporting a David Mellor haircut, bright red bowling shoes and a huge pot belly. He marched up and down, consulted the map, regarded the offending article and declared that yes, it was a pipe. The next question was how our connection to the offending pipe 20 yards away was to be made - this question was greeted by much in-taking of breath and sucking of teeth.

Monsieur Coufignal considered a while and then announced that the town of Cordes was more than happy to take on board the cost of buying a manhole cover but it would be up to me to dig the trench, make the connections, close the road, repave the street, build a replica of the pyramid of Geeza out of sugar cubes, etc.

Just for fun, I suggested that we try and put all the other services in the trench at the same time. I may as well have suggested improper relations with a recently deceased relative. For my pains, I have received a form to fill out, not in triplicate, but in tenplicate, a copy of which is to be sent to anybody who may possibly have any connection to anything that may be buried in said road. Does anybody know any unemployed moles, about the diameter of a sewer pipe?

Boxing Moves

It is finally happening. After months and weeks of frantic trans-Channel phone calls and faxes we have finally sold off our flat in the UK and are teetering on the brink of French home ownership.

Contrary to popular belief, the French administration side has been a breeze compared to trying to get an English solicitor to answer her phone. Our anxiety was compounded by the weight of the hefty non-refundable deposit sitting over our heads like the sword of Damocles. This deposit is compulsory and will be given to the seller if you should pull out of the purchase for any reason less serious than loss of limbs or death, and purchase depended on the rapid sale of the flat in the UK.

This should not have been a problem as we agreed to buy the new house on the same day that our tenants decided to buy from us, plenty of room for manoeuvre as we were given three months to complete over here and were told that the UK sale would take five weeks. In the quick-fire UK marketplace the solicitors managed to complete within ten weeks, the money changers managed to lose £30,000, which they eventually found when I suggested that they look under all the chairs before I took a flight and started turning their office upside down myself.

We finally received the cheque for the money that we need today,

Tuesday, and we have the final signing on Friday.

In contrast to the English hare, the French tortoise moved more like a scalded cat. The French solicitor had all the paperwork ready six weeks ago and the bank was nothing short of miraculous. The French banking system is normally as smoothly oiled as a sack of sand but for some inexplicable reason they managed to sort out my mortgage within two weeks of my request, and in the middle of August when they should all have been on holiday.

The upshot of all of this joyous and expensive fun has been that we have started morphing the contents of our lives into box shapes. Sue has taken it upon herself to put anything that is not bolted down into a box. Some things such as an espresso maker you are not going to miss for at least six months, if at all. Others, such as the cats, you start to miss after not seeing them for a couple of days.

The house now looks like a holding depot for Pickfords and was not perhaps the most welcoming site for our friends who have come to stay from the UK, but they didn't seem to notice the boxes after a couple of bottles of wine, except for the ones that they tripped over. Our conversations have been punctuated by the hackneyed phrase 'But Sue has already packed that.'

Prefaced by 'You could borrow the road map...you could drink that wine out of a glass rather than a mug...' etc.

The good news about their arrival, besides the fact that we were so pleased to see them (honestly), was that they came by car, with a mini-fridge plugged into the cigarette lighter filled to bursting with a block of mature cheddar cheese that could sink a battleship. We would have been so happy if only we could have found a damned knife to cut it with. I wonder which box...?

Chateau To Go

Life as a builder is many things, frustrating, sometimes loss-making, heart lifting, heartbreaking - but never dull.

This is partly due to the huge variety of different types of projects, which come your way. In the two years that I have been here I have tackled barns, farmhouses, townhouses, listed buildings, outhouses and piles of rubble that could barely be called a house at all.

After a while you become slightly blasé. The first derelict building that you see is intimidating, the second is not so bad, and by the time you get to the third you don't worry about anything - you just ask the client which end of the derelict room that they want the TV and get on with it.

So it was with relative sang-froid that I went to visit the latest project to come my way. The prospective client warned me that it was big. I've seen 'big' before; not worried.

I followed the directions and pitched up at the house in the old Escort van that I brought all the way from the homeland.

I use the word 'house' because it is a place that people live in - but the word does not even begin to describe it. The place was enormous. It is probably fair to call it a chateau. It stands in 50 acres and is a derelict slate-roofed beautiful pile with a turret.

The owners were full of boundless enthusiasm for their project, which featured 10 or so bedrooms and countless bathrooms and anterooms. The interior was just like Miss Havisham's house in Great Expectations; somebody had moved out 20 or 30 years ago and everything was exactly as it had been, but dusty and crumbling away. The owners have probably caught the building just in time, before it gets beyond salvation (or worse still, before somebody starts to renovate it badly with UPVC windows).

Even my jaded palette was tempted by the huge potential, and their enthusiasm was just too infectious. I began to understand how they made their fortune in marketing.

A sensible part of me tried to tell myself that the scale was just too big for me and that I didn't have enough time to take on a project like that. I decided to walk away for the time being and go back in the cold light of the following day.

The next day arrived. As I was getting ready to leave the house I said "Sue - I'm not going to take it on; it's just too much work."

I prepared my speech, turned up on site, started talking, got drawn in and four hours later I heard somebody who looked just like me saying "Yes, I'm pretty confident that we can start work in the New Year; we'll soon have this place looking ship-shape." I realised that it was actually my mouth that all of this was spouting from.

Oh well, unless they turn down my quote it looks like I could be spending a lot of time in cloud chateau land. Anybody fancy a job - for life?

Chilled Out

I think that we have been experiencing one of those phenomena that allegedly happen nearly every year, but nobody knows exactly what it is; namely, an Indian summer.

All through September and well into October the south west of France has been bathed in thermometer-busting sunshine. Shorts have not been put away for winter and swimming pools have stayed open.

This has been a particular bonus for us as we were a month late moving into our new home and feared that we had lost the benefit of the summer. We were enjoying a bonanza; that is, until the in-laws hit the tarmac.

Sue's brother, his wife, his baby as well as his sister-in-law had decided to pay us a flying visit and profit from the sunshine. Good plan. But as with the best-laid plans of mice and men it had a major flaw: they were geared up for hot weather.

As the plane hit the ground the clouds descended with it. The mercury in the thermometer fell like a stone and the rain came down. It rained, then it rained, and then it rained some more. The water in the swimming pool dropped from 20 degrees to a hyper-chilly 14 degrees that wouldn't have been inviting in August.

We tried everything, including going out and braving the elements, but it was just not going to work. The rain in this area comes fresh from the Atlantic via the Pyrenees and is cold and very heavy. We were stuck in the house, five adults steadily getting on each other's nerves and a baby that was not at all impressed.

We tried card games, but couldn't find one that everybody knew. We tried my usual solution for boring wet Sundays, cracked the beer open before midday; this did help, but only a bit. The Big Brother challenge of five adults in close proximity almost reached a flash point when I was accused of frying aubergines in a loud manner while the baby was trying to sleep.

No matter how many times we told them how hot it had been a couple of days ago, they didn't believe us. Several dull days later a slightly damp and disgruntled bunch of non-suntanned holidaymakers were ferried back to the airport and discharged back to the UK. Miracle of miracles, the clouds lifted, the sun shone and the temperature belted way back up to the 20s.

What could I say when they phoned later? Should I lie and say that it is still miserable, or should I tell the truth? They probably wouldn't believe the truth, so discretion being the better part of valour, I said nothing and set about putting the chairs back outside, turning the heating off and putting away the woolly jumpers.

I'm sure that there is a moral to be learned from this sorrowful tale of woe, and it is probably that you should never believe a word that anybody tells you. If you are heading into a heatwave, then be sure to you're your wellies and a jumper. And never fry aubergines unless you have a sound proofed room to do it in.

Held to Account

The evil, bloodsucking, spawn of the devil called me the other day. He is also known as le comptable, or the accountant to you or I.

He is actually a very nice chap who goes by the name of Thierry - perhaps more accurately spelt as teary, because that is the way that I usually feel after talking to him.

Being a self-employed small trader, I am obliged to use an accountant to look after my tax affairs and TVA (VAT). This is not because the task is particularly complicated but just because the tax return at the end of the year is about the size of a telephone directory and about as much fun to read. It is structured in such a way that the only person able to negotiate it is the aforementioned comptable.

This would perhaps not be quite so galling if they did not feel the need to charge at least four times as much as their UK counterpart.

But feel the need they do, and they charge like a wounded rhino. When challenged about this latter-day Dick Turpinism, they just give the Gallic shrug and suggest that you try the next guy down the road - you can bet your last centime that he will just charge the same. Why? Because he can and everybody else does, that's why.

Anyway, forgive my spleen, it needed venting. The thrust of his telephone call was to inform me that the French VAT man owed me 3,500 Euros. This was good news and it very nearly cushioned the blow of his six-monthly bill of 1,500 Euros - but not quite.

Despite spitting, swearing and resisting the temptation to put the half-masticated green lizard that the cat had left on the doorstep in the envelope along with the cheque, I sent it away and reflected on my good luck to be a couple of thousand Euros to the good.

My euphoria was typically short lived. The next piece of post to come my way was a bill from URSSAF - this is the French version of the Gestapo but without the humour or manners, masquerading as the people who collect the cash for the hospitals.

Everybody tells me how wonderful the French health service is. I don't care - I never go to the doctor, I don't even know where the nearest one is. I only visit hospitals when somebody points a gun at my head. They don't interest me.

That is, they didn't interest me until I got a demand from URSSAF to pay 9,000 Euros for their upkeep - that is about £6,000 for something that I don't even want. I now understand why the French are such a bunch of hypochondriacs - they are just trying to get value for money. Add that to that the demand for 3,000 Euros that I have just paid towards retirement - I'll be eligible for that after I have paid in for 40 years - I'll buy every Frenchman a Pastis with the first pension cheque that I cash on my 78th birthday, not to mention the many thousands that I pay towards the social fund to pay for the children, what children? I haven't got any.

And there you have a recipe for bankruptcy. Bankruptcy under the sun, still wearing a T-shirt in November with plenty of cheap red wine, c'est la vie.

Winter 2004

Burning Down the House

Moving into somebody else's dream home is a strange business that often throws up more questions than answers.

Did the previous owner of our home have a taste bypass-frontal lobotomy, or did he have a pathological fear of plastered walls that could only be alleviated by covering every single flat surface with tongue and groove pine cladding? His addiction to wood cladding was so strong that when he wallpapered the hallway he used wood effect wallpaper that looks just like the real thing (as if that is a plus).

Don't get me wrong, I like to see a bit of timber as much as the next person, but you can have way too much of a good thing - when you visit the smallest room in the house you can truly imagine how Alec

Guinness felt when the Japs threw him into that sweat box next to the river Kwai.

Japanese torture room meets a Scandinavian sauna house cum ski lodge is probably a fair summary - in fact the chalet look is enhanced by two huge fireplaces with wood-burning stoves. As I sat there looking at the empty fireplaces and across to the walls and ceilings, I had a small epiphany, a moment of clarity: why not marry the two together?

No, I don't mean cladding the fireplaces. Instead of bringing in fuel from outside, why not heat the house from within? Let the bad taste consume itself in flames.

Before you could say Jack Flash the walls were being laid bare, exposing the plaster beneath, and the pine was releasing kilowatts of heat and disappearing up the chimney. Unfortunately this kind of activity is rather addictive and my roving eye fell upon the hideous dark wood kitchen that we had been planning to get rid of. Before I could get a grip upon myself I had dismantled the whole kitchen, kept a couple of units to go in the utility room and was busy shovelling drawer fronts and cupboards onto the fire, handles, hinges and all. Not taking the time to remove the ironmongery did prove to be a small mistake - when Sue cleaned out the three tonnes of ashes the next day she discovered that all the metalwork had welded itself into one massive handle on the grate.

The cold light of day showed me the enormity of my impetuous actions. I had now committed myself to fitting a new kitchen, doing up the utility room and making good the plasterwork. I made a resolution - I would burn what was left of the kitchen, minus handles, slowly and would limit myself to burning one room at a time.

I did start to reflect on what the next owners after us would make of our love for flat plastered walls and our lack of pine cladding. Would they dismiss us as insane? If they are the kind of people who beat themselves with birch branches and eat sushi while skiing downhill, then probably yes.

Each time I now walk up the hardwood staircase that the previous owner paid a fortune for, and which was designed for a house with significantly more headroom (I have the bumps to prove it), I can't help imagining how well it would burn. If only Sue hadn't hidden the chainsaw.

It's a Breeze

The tail end of November finds me, and my faithful retainer Guillaume, in the middle of another barn conversion, once again for an English couple, and once again up to our necks in muck and bullets.

The only real problem with barn conversions at this time year is ventilation. By their very nature barns do lean rather heavily towards ventilation, and plenty of it. If there is anything more than a light breeze, you need to be wearing heavy shoes to keep your toes on the ground.

Having spent many a long English winter hanging off scaffolding in the cold and drizzle, I have to say that a little breeze doesn't worry me too much. Guillaume, on the other hand, is suffering; he is wearing more clothes than a man his size can physically support and is shivering uncontrollably.

Lunchtime was the breaking point for him - I got the deckchairs out, placed them in the middle of the windy barn and offered him a cup of tea. I could tell by the way that he was huddled down inside his coat and looking like an aristocrat in front of Madame Guillotine that he was not a happy bunny.

In one of those cruel twists of fate, the barn that I am converting, a 40-minute drive away, lies approximately two minutes away from where

I used to live until a couple of months ago. Next door, in fact, to Guillaume's house.

In a rare moment of sensitivity to Gallic frailty I did the decent thing and suggested that perhaps he might be happier if we went to his house for lunch and sat in the warm. I have never seen anybody look so grateful. He has, after all, by now accepted the short lunch break and tea instead of coffee, so it was the least I could do.

As we sat in his centrally heated kitchen, we got to talking about the things that we find bizarre about each others culture. We started talking about wine...... a subject about which I know slightly more than nothing. I follow the philosophy of an ancient mariner friend of mine and drink for effect rather than taste. It turns out that the thing about the English and wine that the French find most bizarre is that they drink the stuff on its own.

The idea of a glass of wine being consumed in this way is anathema to your average Frenchman. Apparently wine is only supposed to be consumed with food. The only people, it seems, who enjoy wine without food are the al fresco imbibers that you find on park benches with urine stains on their trousers.

This means, then, that all of these ex-pat middle class wine connoisseurs who spend countless days sat on their terraces being authentically French, drinking bottle after bottle of wine, are destroying our national image. Or more precisely, they are reinforcing a stereotype started by the lager louts: we are now seen as a nation of George Best-a-likes.

This doesn't even begin to touch upon the image of an Englishwoman who goes into a bar and orders a glass of red wine. She may as well hang a red neon light around her neck, sit in an Amsterdam window and swig meths from the bottle. I guess it serves me right for asking. Tomorrow, Guillaume can sit in the draught while I drink a bottle of Thunderbird wine from a brown paper bag.

Into the Groove

When I am king of the world, one of the very first laws that I am going to pass is one banning the use of tongue and groove panelling. No exceptions.

I will burn down all shops selling it and pass severe sentence on anybody even contemplating the use of it.

We have diligently stripped acres of this accursed pine monstrosity from the walls of our new home, but have left it on the ceiling. We have opted for the hat and dark glasses solution..... you can't get rid of it but you can at least hide it with a coat of paint.

Easier said than done of course. First you have to paint the grooves, then roller it and then paint it again, then roller it again, until all you can see in front of your eyes is grooves, and then more grooves. Our latest project at home is to banish the dreaded pine, which has turned that awful dirty tea colour, and to bring in light to our new kitchen-dining room. This small project has turned into a wall-and-chimney-demolishing, tile-lifting, re-plastering, re-plumbing, rewiring monster of a job.

With an impeccable sense of timing, I invited my mum out to stay for her annual visit this week. What better time for a visitor than when you have no kitchen, dust everywhere and complete pandemonium? There has been no shortage of work for her to do, but she keeps on making some lame excuse about recovering from two broken kneecaps, as if this is a reason not to mix concrete.

Do you really need knees to wield a shovel or paint a ceiling? I don't think so. If she hadn't arrived with a suitcase full to bursting with chocolate Hob-Nobs and tea bags, I would have put her straight back on the plane.

Fuelled by cups of tea supplied by my mum (okay, she does have some uses), work has gone on apace. Walls have been made good, trenches in the kitchen have been filled back in and the floor has been levelled ready for tiling.

The trenches in the floor needed filling with concrete, and the only sand that we had for mixing was a large pile lately used by the furry fiends as a litter tray. Mixing this was not one of the greatest pleasures in the world, and now the main active ingredient in our floor is cat nuggets - lighter than standard pebbles, but a lot smellier.

The kitchen arrived from Hygena today, manufactured in the UK and sold all over France in a thousand flat pack boxes. These are all sat in the garage waiting for Sue to grab hold of a screwdriver and try to start making sense of it all.

To my mind, it seems like a perfect job for a mature lady with two dodgy knees. I'll even carry the boxes up from the garage for her to make life a little easier. Perhaps I can start a little production line: I stack the boxes in front of my mum, mum makes the cupboards up, Sue puts them in place, I drink beer in the corner. Dream on.

New Years' Eve Vache

The New Year came in with more of a moo than a bang. This was largely due to the massive bovine, replete with horns, that decided to use our garden as a grazing patch on New Years' Eve.

Having spent most of my life as a town dweller I was somewhat at a loss as to how to deal with a ton of cow that was not in the place where it is supposed to be: ie, behind somebody else's fence.

Sue was quite unfazed by the situation, happily chatting in fluent cow French and accompanied by a curious cat. This started to worry me. I was not bothered about the cow pats or the trampling of plants, I was more worried about Sue getting attached to the damned great big lump. I am already marginalised by the four cats - displaced from chairs and forced to sleep in the one-sixteenth of the bed that doesn't have cats on it. What hope would I have against a cow?

The only thing for it was to try and find a neighbour. We have been in our new home for over three months and I still have not seen a neighbour in our little hamlet, so I decided to take the bull by the horns, as it were.

I started knocking on doors and found our only living neighbour - a typical house-coated little old lady called Camille. She was delighted to see me; I wondered, in fact, if I was her first visitor of 2004. In fact, she was so pleased that she dusted off an old bottle of pastis just for me.

I tried to refuse the drink (this was about 11 in the morning) and told her that all I needed was a number for the farmer. Then I decided not to be churlish and accept her hospitality. We went through the usual niceties. I told her my name, Trevor, and she asked me what it meant. How do you reply to that? It doesn't mean anything much, it just is what it is. I am rather hampered by having a name unknown in French that has no famous holders. If you are called Brad you just say Brad Pitt and you are away. Say Trevor and they just look at you as if you are an idiot, perhaps with good reason.

I explained about the cow and I got the sense that she didn't really believe me. She insisted on coming back to the house with me to see for herself. Lo and behold: it really was a cow.

A call was made and an elderly farmer with his equally elderly bobble-hatted wife squelched up. (I know farmers always complain about not having any money, but I would have thought that a leaky Wellington could be replaced, rather than resorting to a carrier bag as a liner.) Armed with a stick and bandy legs they chased Daisy out of our gates and on to pastures new, leaving us cowless but having gained a neighbour that we never knew existed.

At least I know where to go for a free drink now.

January is not so taxing in rural France

January in the deepest, darkest corner of rural France brings with it a fair measure of pleasure and pain for the English minority that has to work for a living.

The first pain is the aching and creaking muscles that return to work after relaxing and indulging over the festive holiday. This is tempered by seeing the happy, smiling faces of the clients who have loved having no builders creating dust, dirt and mayhem for a couple of weeks.

The true pleasure begins when we once again commence creating dust, dirt and mayhem, bringing chaos where once there was order.

A pleasure for Sue is the January sales. These are quite spectacular in France, to the extent that the shops close the day before in order to prepare. The pain to the wallet is obvious, but apparently the pleasure for me lies in Sue's pleasure.

A lingering pleasure for us lies in seeing the Christmas lights strung across the streets and upon the street lamps. Even a tiny town like ours makes a big splash in the Christmas light stakes. The pleasure will just go on and on, because the norm over here appears to be to leave the decorations up until they rot or explode into a ball of flames. The hugest pain for everybody in France is the annual tax return. They all have to be done at the beginning of January for everybody. This is organised expressly by the French Government so that all the civil servants can be insanely busy for the two dullest months of the year, January and February, when there is nothing much else to do. This means that they can spend the other 10 months of the year taking lunch breaks, starting late, going on holiday and attending to their mistresses. The pleasure lies in writing them a big fat cheque for doing nothing.

The searing pain of the moment comes from the early-morning sub-zero temperatures, the frozen roads, the freezing fog, suicidal deer running in front of the van and the breaking of the ice on the water butt to mix mortar with frozen sand.

To every Yin there must be a Yang, and the Yang arrives every day at around 10 o'clock when the fog dissipates, the ice defrosts and you can see for miles beneath the clear blue skies.

By the afternoon the mercury heads up to the high 20s, and a cup of tea while you are sat on a scaffold clad in a T-shirt can be a truly sublime January moment.

If the price of a pleasure such as that is a little pain, then I say, bring on the tax forms - I can take it.

The Clients

The telephone rings at nine o'clock on Sunday morning. There are not many things that warrant a telephone call at that time on a Sunday; the news of a distant millionaire aunt dying and leaving you her fortune is a candidate, but even an invite to a debauched day of wine and fun beside a pool in summer is not welcome at that time.

Imagine my delight when I picked up the receiver and a chirpy voice said "Hi Trevor, I hope I didn't wake you up, my shower tray is leaking."

This was a man that I had met a few days before to discuss the possibility of renovating the barn that he had just bought. He was over here for a short visit with his wife and children.

Nearly struck dumb with incredulity, I actually managed to explain that although he had not actually woken me, he had got me out of bed and that was just as bad. Water off a duck's back. He went on to explain how the water was dripping all over the place and could I sort it out, as he was off back to the UK. Clicking in to automatic, I politely said for him not to worry about it and to leave it with me.

It was not until I put the phone down that I nearly had an apoplectic fit about the cheek of somebody calling me on a Sunday to sort out a leak on an appliance that I didn't fit, especially when he wasn't even a client as yet. I wouldn't even bother sorting out my own shower tray on a Sunday. I was supposed to care about his?

He went by the name of Treadwell. More like tread carefully or you'll be looking for another builder, matey. The alarm bells should really have rung during our first meeting when we were walking around the vast barn that needs 90 per cent demolishing before his dream home can rise like a phoenix from the ashes.

His dream home is currently an idea in his and his wife's minds, probably containing a wet room and granite work surfaces, all the rest just being mere details. With no firm plan, let alone any architect's drawings, he asks me how much it will cost.

How on earth are you supposed to reply to a question like that? I doubt if he would walk into a car dealership and ask how much it costs to buy a car, not knowing if he wanted a basic Mini or a top of the range Aston Martin.

If it hadn't been for the fact that his daughter made me a cup of tea, I would have walked away there and then. Added to that the fact that I was feeling charitable because he had made me laugh when he explained that he could fit me in for a site meeting just after the architect and before his visit to Ikea.

His architect turned up an hour and a half late, and I knew his visit to

Ikea would be hell. People on a tight time schedule soon learn that things don't quite go according to plan in France. For example, a barn renovation can suddenly cost 20 per cent more when you factor in the builder's broken leisure time on a Sunday spent talking on the phone. Could be his dearest phone call yet.

Breaking Out

What is it about us Brits that makes us completely unable to leave things well alone?

Your average Frenchman is perfectly capable of decorating the interior of a house and then living quite comfortably with the fruits of his labours for the rest of his natural life. His offspring will move in after he dies and also be quite happy.

This 'being happy with things as they are' gene appears to be missing from us Brits. If things are one way, we have to have them another, and the idea of living with the same colour on the walls for longer than the average life of a Mayfly brings us out in a rash. So it was that we decided to take our perfectly habitable four-bedroom, one-bathroom house and turn it into a three-bedroom, two-bathroom house.

Step one: get the boys around. This took the form of myself, Guillaume my erstwhile colleague and Darryn the brain-damaged electrician.

Darryn was a computer programmer until he was hit on the back of the head by a huge hailstone and rendered incapable of focusing on a computer screen for long periods of time. Brain damage ideally qualified him for following a French wiring layout. He has been doing all of my wiring installations since I gave our last psychotic electrician his marching orders after he punched a hole in one too many walls. The boys arrived early in the morning and Sue departed on a shopping expedition. We had the obligatory cup of tea and then waded in. Sledgehammers flew, walls fell, dust billowed and before you could say what a mess, the upstairs was in pieces.

In order to remove all of the rubble we hitched up the trailer and filled it to the brim. All that was left to do was to drive it down our very steep driveway and unload it at the bottom where I had a handy big hole to fill.

I asked Guillaume to move it. He drove very cautiously, stopped and told me that the drive was too slippery and that we would have to reverse down.

Not being very well known for my patience, I told him not to be so stupid and that I would move it. He shrugged.

I jumped into the van, gunned the engine and off I went. Everything was fine, no problems - at least until I touched the brakes. A heavy weight pushing a van down a slippery drive does funny things under braking.

Before I knew what was happening the van was sliding sideways and the trailer was attempting to overtake me. Darryn and Guillaume were diving for safety and my life was flashing in front of my eyes.

The man who we bought the house from might have made a bit of a hash of the room layouts but I'm damned glad that he planted that laurel hedge along the side of the drive. It was the only thing that stopped me ending up at the bottom of the Averyon gorge under a pile of twisted metal and rubble.

The worst thing about it was having to tell Guillaume that he was right. That hurt.

Butterflies

There are times when you are grappling with a foreign tongue (as in language, that is) when you become completely exasperated with the complexities of it all and feel the need to pass a European decree forcing all nationalities to speak English.

And then there are other times when the lilt and charm of the French language just trips off the tongue and skips through the meadows. One such phrase which struck me between the eyes was when I asked my colleague how he felt about something, or how he was feeling, he replied "Heureux comme un papillon."

This literally translates as 'happy as a butterfly', and presumably not a Papillon that has just been sentenced to life imprisonment on the penal colony of Devil's Island.

This phrase conjures up visions of happy butterflies floating through summer pastures, and seems in no way similar to the nearest English equivalent of happy as a sandboy.

What is a sandboy? Have you ever met one? How has he come to be a measure of the state of happiness?

There was a certain incongruity to my colleague's phrase, however, given our present conditions. We are in the middle of a bone-cracking, pipe-bursting, mercury-freezing cold spell which makes the UK seem like the tropics by comparison.

Night-time temperatures are regularly plummeting to minus 9 or 10 degrees. The drips on the end of your nose freeze as you walk from the van to the site.

One of my sites is an old building that hasn't been blessed with doors and windows since at least the beginning of the last century, and at the present rate of progress won't be getting any until the next. This lack of glazing means that the building stores up all of the cold of the night before and gradually releases it during the day, like a storage heater in reverse. When the milk froze and tea was off the menu, an agreed walkout was the only solution.

It is an ill wind that blows no good, and there is an upside. It has meant that we spent a bit of time working on my own house. This has had mixed effects on the lovely Sue. She has been papillon-like about men around the house busy wiring, building, plastering and creating the rooms of her dreams, and decidedly unpapillon about the noise, dust, debris, traumatised cats and all that stuff that follows builders around.

In fact, she is beginning to speak like a real client, saying things like "It will be nice when it is finished."

This really translates as, "I can't wait until these bloody builders leave." I did point out that I was one of the bloody builders and perhaps she wouldn't want me to leave. She made no comment.

I remain positive. I just know that as soon as the dust settles and the house of her dreams emerges, she will be one very heureuse papillon.

Spring 2005

Confessional

I have a small confession to make. I have just fallen foul of that noblest of French traditions, the long arm of the law.

The day started harmlessly enough. I had to go to our regional capital of Montauban to re-register my business (we have moved departments and therefore have to register all over again). This onerous task was filling me with dread. Having jumped through burning hoops the first time to register, the idea of doing it again was only just above a trip to the dentist on my wish list.

I have just bought a new van, we've bought a new bed minus the mattress and Sue was at a loose end. Put them all together and you have the makings of a fun-filled day out for all the family.

The first task was to find the Chambre des Métiers, they are usually well hidden, this helps the artisan to waste the whole day on a visit, rather than just a half. The secretaries who stand station at the front desk are not dissimilar to the two-headed dogs that guard the gates of Hades, except they can be a little bit more vicious - especially if you have forgotten one of the vital pieces of paper that keeps the bureaucratic wheels revolving at a snail's pace.

This first task was made easy by some helpful directions from a friendly gendarme. Success, in through the door, surprise, no queue, incredulity, a friendly secretary, jaw-dropping disbelief, the whole thing dealt with and a brand new identity card in my sweaty mitt in under 15 minutes.

My shock rendered me barely able to string the words together to thank her for her help, and to tell her how incredibly efficient she was. If you don't offer a little praise you don't have the right to criticise, and seeing as I criticise in spades, praise I did, and put myself in credit.

Walking on cloud nine, we went out to the van. A quick look at the watch told us that we had plenty of time to get to the mattress shop before noon closing.

We pulled away, my phone rang, and I answered it. The two last items are a bit unusual in themselves - my phone rarely rings. I'm a bit of a Billy No Mates in the world of modern communications. I don't bother much with talking on the phone, therefore nobody phones me and I don't talk on the phone when I am driving.

Today was an exception. Guillaume was phoning me to tell me that he was back from the Alps - too much snow, like I should care - and before you could say 'go to jail' I was pulled over by the Municipal Police and having every piece of paper remotely connected to piloting a vehicle inspected in minute detail.

If you are one of those people who thinks that the blue flag with the stars in it on your licence means that it is an EU licence, think again. I got a roasting for talking on the phone; a roasting for not having a French licence and three weeks to sort out the situation. The phone is easy to remedy - chuck it in the nearest bin - but the licence is a bit more complicated. I have to get a medical certificate stating that I am competent (a tall order), and photocopies of every piece of identity that I have ever had.

Climbing back into my van, head held low in shame, I was offered words of comfort by Sue. "You idiot, you have just been stopped by the Municipal Police - not even the proper gendarmes with their guns and sexy leather boots, and one of them was a girl. In fact, a real chick flic."

What could I say? It was a fair cop - bring on the handcuffs.

The Hospital Job

I'm going to let you into a little trade secret, one of those secret things that builders are not allowed to tell to Joe Public, on pain of death. This secret is the 'hospital job'. This is the job that you keep in reserve, the job that you go to when every other job that you have has been postponed, cancelled or gone belly-up.

You may be the proprietor of a hospital job if you kindly said to the builder, "Fit us in when you can," or if you pushed so hard for a price reduction that the job is hardly worth doing now, or if you are just a plain old horrible customer. I'm sorry to say it, but they do exist.

My particular hospital job was a derelict town house in a medieval quarter. The reason it became a hospital job is two-fold; firstly, it had to be done for a bargain price, and secondly, nobody is going to live in it until the next holiday season so we are fitting it in when we can. A corresponding lull before the coming storm has given me a few weeks to finish off what I started six months ago. This fits in with the ball that I started rolling some time ago to get water, electricity, sewers and telephone connected to a building that has never known any of the aforementioned.

This involved contacting every known available supplier of anything that goes into a house, filling out forms aplenty, meeting representatives of all the services and generally trying to juggle jelly in order to get everybody to come at the same time and put everything into the same trench.

There were times along this journey that I almost gave up, but bloody-minded obstinacy and a need to put in the final bill stopped these negative inclinations.

In the words of Chairman Mao: "A thousand-mile march begins with just one step," or something like that. In this way, the final destination finally came into sight this Monday.

Firstly the trench diggers turned up with their mini digger - we were sent the elderly crew in various states of decay, but very friendly and cheerful.

They were followed by the electric guy (armed with digital photos showing him where to stick his box), followed by the water man, followed by the telephone man, followed by the representative of the council works department to make sure that we weren't going to mess up his town.

On this last point I would have to say that we have made a bit of a mess - 20 metres of trench down an 800-year-old cobbled street does probably count as a bit of a mess, but it will soon be repaired. The moral of this story has to be that perseverance will always pay off. Bang your head against that brick wall for long enough and it will eventually give way, spend long enough in the hospital and you'll get better, spend long enough dealing with the French system and you will still never get to understand how it works.

Has anybody seen my nurse?

What's Up Doc?

A trip to the see the doctor is, in my opinion, something that should be avoided at all costs. I would generally wait until my leg had actually fallen off before I would go and see one of our white-coated friends.

So I was not terribly happy when I found myself in the unfortunate position of having to make an appointment. My malady was not so much one of physical ill health. It was more the consequence of terminal stupidity. I had been stopped by the gendarmes for talking on the phone while driving and was thus obliged to surrender my UK driving licence and take a French one.

This appeared not to be quite so bad as I had feared. There was to be no re-test, a damned good thing too, as anyone would testify who ever had to sit in a car with me. The downside was that I had to have a medical. I made the appointment and dutifully turned up at the appointed time.

The waiting room was decorated in Baroque-meets-Hansel-and-Gretel style. Its eerie silence was shattered when the door to the surgery was thrown open and a supremely bald Boris Karloff-alike emerged. He screamed at me and the other poor unfortunate next to me: "Is there an Anglais?" Before I had a chance to confess he jabbed his finger at me and said "It's you, isn't it?"

Unable to deny my origins, I confessed all and stood up. He grabbed my arm and threw me into the consulting room, pushed me towards a chair and told me, in no uncertain terms, to sit down. I tried to make some pleasantries about how I had come to be in the unfortunate position of having to be there; I was cut dead.

"How tall are you?" he yelled. I had to confess that I had no idea of my height in the metric system. I was told to stand up while he stared at me and guessed my height. The same procedure with my weight, except that I had to lift my shirt to show that I was not too fat. The questions became more intensive and even more carefully measured. I was asked if I could hear OK; as I answered yes, that box was ticked. I also answered in the affirmative to the question about whether or not I could see things. The matter of my peripheral vision was sorted out when he approached me, stuck two fingers beside my head, slapped me in the face and asked "How many?"

He gave me a clue that the consultation was over by reaching into his wallet and taking out 25 Euros, pointing at the money and saying "You....me...give."

Cheap at the price, I thought, scribbled out a cheque as fast as I could and got up to leave. Before I could make more than one step towards the door that I had come through, I was spun around and pushed out of the French doors into the garden and left to find my own way out through the undergrowth.

What can I say? If an apple a day keeps the doctor away, I'm planting an orchard tomorrow.

Getting Wrecked

Ever being a sucker for a sad story and also being a man to repay his debts, I found myself, trowel in hand, at the house of my brain-damaged electrician colleague.

I use the word 'house' in the loosest possible sense. Darryn and Jackie had fallen in love and committed themselves to a classic French property. The building is a standard L-shaped old farmhouse and its dependences with all the attendant charms and pitfalls: the stone, the draughts, the huge floor areas and therefore the huge areas to be renovated.

He had lent me a hand with the electrics on my house. This had been deemed necessary because my idea of trimming an electric cable generally involves a disc cutter closely followed by a long period of darkness for all properties in the vicinity. Builders and electricity do not mix.

Payback time arrived and I was called in. His wife has been catering for themselves and two young boys on one table, loosely described as a kitchen, getting the water for washing-up from the bathroom and wearing three jumpers to keep out the cold blowing in from the barn below which should really be a kitchen.

It was my task to try and get the project back on course. It was suffering from the standard problem of just too much to be done. Motivation drops when the task is too large. In order to get the kitchen thing moving we needed some floors, so we levelled out the piles of rubble, phoned for the concrete delivery man, poured floors throughout and scored a small victory.

Next of all they would need windows. Old barns weren't big on windows, they were seen as a frivolous expense that the animals would never appreciate. The incoming English animals don't see things the same way and want windows aplenty.

Rising to the challenge, four window openings were punched in the two-foot thick stone walls and oak lintels put in place and the beginnings of a room started to take shape.

After all of these wreck-transforming antics a new problem began to rear its ugly head. The works had pushed me well past my debt to the brain-damaged sparks. This has two possible consequences. I could ask him to pay me for my time, but that is not really an option when you are colleagues and friends; money is a thing reserved for clients. The second option is finding more work for him at our place.

As we have nearly finished the major electrical work on the main house we will need to look at other parts. There just happens to be garage attached to the house that has no floor or particular purpose in life; it is just crying out to be turned into a home cinema, and that will need electricity. Isn't that just always the way... you try to help ease the burden on somebody else and what happens? You just end up making more work for yourself.

Still, not to worry, even if their kitchen never gets finished, they can always come over to ours to watch a film - maybe Mr Blanding Builds His Dream Home.

Barnstorming

This week has been a bit of a groundbreaker, in more ways than one. It has seen the arrival of my first bona fide French clients since I started my building renovation business nearly two years ago - I have never advertised and have just let the business grow through word of mouth.

As my first clients were English and the English community talks amongst itself, the obvious has happened and all my clients have been English, but all of that is changing. I am now crossing boundaries and my first clients take the shape of Danielle and Patrick.

Danielle is a tubby, gravely-voiced Parisienne married to Patrick, who is every inch your standard moustachioed Frenchman, from his ever present Gaulloise to his rotund belly, fuelled by red wine and Pastis.

They are the in-laws of my good friend and colleague Guillaume, he has sold them an old barn next to his house, and sold them my services into the bargain. They happily signed on the dotted line for the barn of their dreams, sold their home on the outskirts of Paris and moved down to the sunny south west of France in time for Easter.

The one small hitch in this fluffy dream was that we broke ground on the project the week before they arrived, this meant me and Guillaume demolishing the roof and a 10-tonne tracked machine making mincemeat out of all the associated concrete pens, cattle feeders and outbuildings that attach themselves to barns over the years.

This apocalyptic devastation typically coincided with the driest winter in living memory coming to an abrupt end with the onset of a deluge of Biblical proportions, that is not forecast to end for at least another week.

This has transformed a dusty, roofless barn into a hideous quagmire that turns a respectable pair of feet into humungous mud-coloured platform shoes. You can imagine their faces when they arrived after a 10-hour journey down from Paris, to discover the home of their dreams turned into barely three walls and no roof. They took this on the chin, with admirable restraint, and obviously thought that things could only get better - until I arrived to start work this week and promptly smashed a gaping hole in on of the remaining walls that was still intact, to create a doorway.

I could see that they were putting a brave face on things, but not truly believing that the gaping mud-filled hole could ever become such a thing as a kitchen. There is not much point in platitudes, you just have to let them see the results for themselves, and results there will have to be.

Guillaume's chambres d'hôtes business is next door and is not allowed to have any building work going on in high season (three months' time) and he has rented out the gîte that Danielle and Patrick are staying in at the same time. That puts us somewhere between a pile of rocks and a mud bath, with a shotgun at our backs. Can we succeed? Of course we can - if the French and the English built a tunnel under the Channel, I'm damned sure that we can do up a barn in three months - I hope.

Anglais go Home:
France makes its feelings clear on Britons who grate

There are ominous rumblings abroad, thunder clouds are gathering and threatening to burst, spilling forth rivers of ex-pat blood in the streets and alleyways.

Hundreds of wine-soaked has-beens, never-weres and might-have-beens are going to be seized by their paysan neighbours and herded off to meet Madame Guilloutine.

Ok, I may be exaggerating very slightly, but the wash of anti-British sentiment that has made itself felt in Brittany has sent ripples down to us.

A local village near us had its signs decked with posters declaring a wish to see all the Brits sent back to their own country; we were blamed for inflated house prices, rural poverty and the sinking of the Rainbow Warrior. (My mistake - that was the French, by a strange coincidence, the mayor of one of our local towns is rumoured to have been a cabinet member when that fateful decision was made.)

The upshot of all this has been a new topic of conversation for the Brits hanging about in cafés. The initial shock of discovering that maybe some people don't like us much has turned into the defensive debate about how the Brits have salvaged rural France.

There is an element of truth in this. Brits have pumped a great deal of cash into renovating old properties, many of which would otherwise have simply crumbled and disappeared. Most French that I have met admire the good taste that the English restore houses with and are pleased that they buy local materials and use local services.

The most disdain is reserved for the Dutch, who import articulated lorries full of building materials and bring their tradesman down from Holland, spending nothing locally.

None of this helps, though, in respect of the attitude of some locals who cannot afford to buy a home in their own village. It is not hard to see their point of view. They work hard for low wages and are pretty hacked off when they see yet another family of rich Brits moving in. (All Brits are seen as rich because the vast majority don't work for a living, despite often being well below retirement age. I must admit that this bugs me as well.)

I suspect that this media-driven storm in a teacup will blow itself out in time, but if it doesn't, the results are perhaps too awful to contemplate. Could the UK cope with the sudden return of boatloads of dispossessed, flower-pressing, interior designing, feckless, navel-contemplating alcoholics?

I suggest that Tony Blair sends funds to the rural French pretty damned quick, or you may find yourselves having to adopt an unwanted Brit.

Les Cowboys

The world is full of woeful tales of dodgy builders who rip off clients - typically taking as much cash as possible upfront and never being heard from again. In that respect, France is no exception.

I am not here to add to these tales of woe, I am here to redress the balance. I am here to tell you about the scourge of the honest artisan: the client.

Although I am prepared to admit that the odd member of the general public is not too bad a person, as soon as they decide to become a client they morph into horned sons of Satan with matching tails.

One of the worst kinds of client is one that will never actually become a client. This is the kind of person that studies the pages jaune and phones every artisan that they can find, luring them to their home with promises of work and riches.... essentially, wasting everybody's time. Equipped with dozens of quotes, this sort of person will deduce that they are all way too expensive, and brings their brother-in-law over form the UK to rebuild a barn. He is well qualified because he once tiled a bathroom.

Another type of client is the eternal ditherer. They call you in and start to convey their plans to transform a cupboard into a full-size bowling alley before abruptly changing tack to tell you about their dreams of hanging gardens in the field below.

It is necessary to beware of these people: they suck you in by making you believe them to be helpless, and before you know it, you have put a large amount of time into preparing drawings and searching high and low for rare materials. If you find yourself cooking their evening meal, you have been sucked in too far.

The very worst kind of cowboy client is the final payment bumper. These people are generally wealthy beyond the dreams of mere mortals, and there is a very good reason for this. They begin by screwing the artisan's price down to the floor with promises of attractive future projects if you do this one for a good price. Not being satisfied with a cheap job, they keep upping the spec, always making sure that more expensive and difficult to use materials are provided at the expense of the poor builder.

They always pay late, there is generally an excuse about money changing, endowment cashing or share selling. They do pay eventually, though, which lulls the builder into the belief that he will always get his money in the end. The rude awakening comes at the end of the job when the final payment is due, because the best way to make a cheap job even cheaper is not to pay the final 30 per cent. Let the builder think that the money is coming - this encourages him to finish the job. When he is finishing off the final brush-up, tell him that the wife cannot live with the particular shade of puce that she chose and is inconsolable, therefore a cheque cannot and will not be forthcoming.

If there is a ring of bitterness about this account, this is because one of my last clients fell into at least two of these categories, and as soon as I can satisfactorily translate the phrase 'threaten to break his kneecaps and eat his liver' to my local hit man the problem should be resolved. Brothers, beware of cowboy clients.

Kicking Off

Springtime has turned right, just after Greenland and sidled its way down to those hard to reach parts of France. This would have been all very well if it hadn't decided to bring those damned April showers with it.

Don't get me wrong, I think that rain is a useful thing, it provides us with water.... sorry, I can't think of anything else good to say about rain. I'll be honest, I hate rain. Having spent my entire working life outside and at the whim of the elements I have come to dread the wet stuff. The building trade depends on water, but only on our terms.

The latest victim, sorry, I mean project has been rather badly prejudiced by inclement weather - the driest winter since the time of the gladiators came to an abrupt end as soon as we demolished the old roof, leading to three-inch platform soles. Not the first time that I have been accused of having feet of clay.

This has led to the need to pour concrete floors throughout. Either we have a working surface to work on or all work stops. On top of this, a delay on roofing materials means that half of the floors are al fresco. A good concrete floor requires plenty of water - as I had ordered three lorry-loads of Ready Mix concrete - several hundred gallons of the wet stuff. All started well at eight o'clock in the morning with the first delivery being poured in the early morning sunshine and continued apace.

I was happily levelling and trowelling and was not even fazed when the last delivery arrived a little bit short. The driver explained that he stopped to talk to somebody when he was on a steep hill and lost several hundred litres of concrete out of the back of the mixer.

He didn't seem too bothered about it, but I don't know how the people behind him took to the unexpected appearance of a new sleeping policeman.

Despite the inconvenience of having to do some mixing ourselves to make up for the shortfall we had all 18 cubic metres levelled by three o'clock and were feeling pleased as punch, admiring the beautiful flat surfaces until Mother Nature decided to turn the billiard table into the surface of the moon.

Thanks a bunch! Not only is the rain fouling up professional operations, it is also playing havoc with the more important preparations for the dual events of the arrival of my big sister with husband and my birthday bash. Sue professes to be excited at the prospect of seeing my sister, but I think that the rumoured two pairs of River Island jeans in her luggage are playing a part.

As part of the preparations, we thought that we ought to tidy up the garden - well, it was a garden until all that damned water came down.

What used to be a barren dustbowl has sprung into dismaying fecundity. Half-inch ground cover has transformed itself into legions of triffids that are threatening to thwart the best efforts of prospective visitors and revellers from finding the driveway, let alone the house at the end of it.

It seems to me as if there is only one solution. Embrace the blessed H2O, I'm going to start with a small dose, some of that tonic water with just a splash of gin - that'll put a spring in my step.

Bonne Fête

Springtime has brought flowers, leaves and weeds springing forth, accompanied by a hefty dose of visitors to our tranquil hilltop hideaway.

The visitors have taken the form of my big sister and her husband. Their visit has been fortuitous in many ways, not least being the scale-busting weight of Cadburys chocolate that they brought over.

The second huge bonus is that my brother-in-law has just taken voluntary redundancy from Westlands and has decided to set up his own gardening business. What better way to start a new business than with your very first international contract?

Skilfully marrying needs and means together, we have strapped him into the strimmer harness and set him off around the garden. He seems perfectly happy and if you put your fingers in your ears he barely disturbs the peace and quiet.

The visitor numbers reached huge proportions last week when we held my 40th-minus-one party bash. People came from far and wide to show their love and affection for me, or maybe it was just the lure of plenty of booze and a boogie.

One of my French guests was horrified at my painstaking lack of precision planning. I had written on the invite that any food and drink contributions would be welcome. This posed a very obvious question in her French mind: "What happens if everybody brings drink and no food?"

The answer to this question was straightforward to anyone of UK extraction: "We drink all the booze and then we'll soon forget that we haven't eaten anything." This response was somewhat less than satisfactory for her, but it did at least spur her on to arrive at the party with her family laden down with bags and boxes full of goodies.

The evening started extremely well with the rum punch being skilfully mixed by me using only the finest ingredients. This did present one small problem: in order to get the mix of fruit juices and Bacardi just right you do have to taste it.

I'm sure that you are ahead of me here. I mixed and I tasted, tasted and mixed, tasted again, forgot about mixing, remembered about mixing, mixed it wrong and you can guess the rest. I place almost all of the blame on the Rhum Agricole. The name should have been a giveaway - and if not then the emphasis placed on the large numbers declaring 55 per cent.

The evening seemed to go off very well and I even managed to MC the presentation of the prestigious Client of the Year Award 2004. This was carefully deliberated upon by myself and my colleagues. The clients had to excel in many areas - among them the mundane ones such as paying their bills, making decisions and not whingeing too much when I blew all their fuses by slicing the power cables with a disc cutter - but mostly for getting up in the morning and putting the kettle on for a cup of tea.

The winner was assisted by the fact that the lady had to make numerous business trips back to the UK and would bring back bars of galaxy for Sue.

The award made them very happy and upset all my other clients, but at least it will make them all try harder for next year.

It Pays to Advertise

The latest addition to the household (for household read menagerie) has been making one hell of a racket.

The newest resident has set himself up in the pond at the back of our house. When I say pond, I really mean the primeval green swamp that looks putrid enough to kill any wildlife that comes in contact with it but somehow manages to host a thriving population of goldfish.

He is a handsome fellow - about the size of your fist with a huge green stripe running down his back, as if he is wearing a cheap shell suit, and he has been keeping us awake all night with his constant croaking.

As you may have guessed, he is a genuine frog, and apparently the reason for his verbal gymnastics was that age-old male search: he was looking for love.

Although I think he is rather handsome I did fear that I was in the minority, and if I were brutally honest I would have to say that he does really have a face that only a mother could love.

Imagine my surprise when I wandered up to the pond and saw that his constant advertising had paid off. He had found himself a girlfriend

- not any old minger from the streets, but a rather pretty young thing. I think it is safe to say that we shall be hearing the splash of little webbed feet pretty soon.

As if that wasn't enough, the Siamese cat that Sue befriended when he pitched up at our door has seriously put on weight. Sue rather imaginatively named him Simon the Siamese but his name is being re-evaluated due to the weight that he has put on being mainly in one place and looking suspiciously like it may turn into a bunch of kittens. This has turned Simon into a Simone.

It must be something about the sudden hot weather that is having an effect. Take the wasps: you can't get much less amorous than a wasp, but they can't be bothered to sting you because they are too busy bothering each other.

Even the little speckled beetles that look a bit like ladybirds are joined back to back and wandering about like pushmepullyou llamas from Dr Doolittle. Thank God that Sue talks to the animals because I'm not really sure what is going on at all.

I think that it is fairly normal for cats to want to sleep on the bed, but I'm not sure that they are supposed to sleep under the duvet stretched out lengthways alongside you.

I may go outside and start croaking a bit - you never know what may come along.

Everyone's a Foreigner

Despite our global isolation, word still gets through to us of events in the outside world.

Word has reached us of your choice of leader over there in UK Land. We even got to hear about some of their reasons for gaining power: something along the lines of "We are dreadful power-hungry egomaniacs, but we are slightly less bad than the others."

Political debates run along pretty much the same lines over here, and there is always, if necessary, that sinister political ace that is often played: the race or immigration card.

This is often a very popular card, enabling an ugly moron such as LePen to clean up more votes than he deserves. It is a debate that actually has a resonance for us now. My gut reaction as an Englishman, despite coming from somewhat mongrel stock, is that I am an Englishman no matter where I am, and it is the rest who are foreign. But after living in somebody else's country for a while and even taking on some of their habits and living their sort of life, you begin to realise that you are not a holidaymaker but an immigrant.

This word conjures up people crammed into refrigeration containers and living in crowded bed-sits, but it applies just as well to the middle classes who smuggle themselves over here in air-conditioned Range Rovers and whose idea of overcrowding is being able to see your neighbour's chimney across the valley.

All of those dinner party criticisms that are so vehemently voiced in suburbia suddenly begin to ring a few home truths. Arriving in a foreign land, it is indeed often more comfortable to settle in a location near others of the same nationality. It is easier to socialise with others from your homeland (though I have heard rumours of Antipodeans being allowed into British homes). And certainly you can spend years in a country without speaking a word of the native tongue. People who don't need to work can manage quite comfortably with never speaking a single word of French; everybody they know is English and you just need to read the monitor to see how many Euros to give the checkout girl at the supermarket.

The criticism levelled against immigrants most commonly is that they scrounge from the state and contribute nothing. Surprisingly, you might think, this holds just as true for the monied immigrants: they of course pay a minimum of tax in their native country, spending large portions of their time pushing money around offshore accounts, and they try to make damned sure that they don't pay a cent to their host country. You should hear them squeal when they get asked to pay capital gains tax on the profit they make from selling their homes over here.

There is of course the flip side. Immigrants have traditionally been a good thing for a country: they can be dynamic, inventive and enthusiastic. (The US did pretty well on a good few million of them.) They bring different cultures and new styles of food with them.

Perhaps, in the end, history will look kindly on us Brits in 21st century France. In 50 years' time, when your average Frenchman is tucking into his slice of Marmite on toast and looking forward to a fried egg sandwich with HP sauce, he may think that it was a damned good idea letting us in after all.

Idiot Savant

There are times when being a congenital idiot can be a bit of a bore. There are other times when it is downright dangerous. One such time was last Friday night.

I was extremely late getting home from site, having been diverted by meeting Sue in Gaillac for a pizza after her eye examination. This had its compensations in the shape of a young waitress with a plunging neckline, a lacy bra and a constant need to bend over. Eyes examined, pizza eaten and face slapped for leching, we made our way home in the van with the trailer in tow.

Let me set the scene. It is 10 o'clock at night, pouring with rain. We live at the top of a very steep hill overlooking the gorges, and I need to unhitch the trailer. Do I really need to say more?

I unhitched the trailer without any problem. Indeed, I had it in my hand. Unfortunately my hands were attached to my body, which was attached to my feet, which were sliding on the wet gravel.

Something had to go, and go it did. I called for Sue to help me but to no avail. Several hundred kilos of trailer were making their first solo trip down the driveway and heading for the laurel hedge (the same one that I once crashed my old van into).

Then a miracle happened. The jockey wheel hit the ground and spun the trailer. The situation was saved as the trailer turned an abrupt 90 degrees. Unfortunately that was only an interlude. It hesitated and then headed down through the orchard, taking out two apple trees in its path. I had visions of it either demolishing the stone pillars at the entrance to the drive or else passing between them and ending up at the bottom of the gorge. The gods smiled, however. It wedged itself against a sturdier specimen of tree, earning me yet another slap from Sue for being an idiot, and a tricky extrication contract.

Fortunately I wasn't the only one in the house to feel a bit foolish this weekend. Ruben, our big fat tabby cat, decided that it might be a good idea to sit by the pool and watch Sue cleaning it. Unfortunately, Milly (the little grey cat that Sue rescued form certain death on a busy road) has a mischievous streak and she thought that it would be good idea to ambush Ruben.

Milly pounced, Ruben jumped, Sue screamed and Ruben found the place that he jumped to a little damp. He was in at the deep end, never having been anywhere wetter than a cloudburst before, and Sue was having kittens.

I know what you are thinking - did it make any difference that it was the deep end?

Call it dramatic effect. Ruben had his first adrenalin rush and learnt to swim in a second and got himself out in one piece. The thing that struck Sue most was that normally when a cat gets wet there is a thin cat living underneath all that fur; not so with Ruben - there is just another fat cat.

Opposing Opposites

It is a strange irony of working life that we spend more waking hours with completely unrelated people to ourselves in the work place than we do with our chosen loved ones. I suppose, though, that this could be seen as a good way of preserving our loved ones as exactly that. My particular opposite number is Guillaume. Despite our sharing certain physical characteristics (slim, dark-haired and devilishly handsome) he is in almost every respect my polar opposite. His glass is perpetually half-empty, whereas mine is always half-full - except on weekends when it always seems to be empty.

I turn up on site in the morning in a blissful state of Zen calm. Guillaume will pitch up in a high state of agitation, having run out of fuel, argued with his neighbour, and lost his wallet or his glasses, or any other one of a 100 catastrophes that can only befall him.

Some of our differences are cultural. He is primarily a Frenchman; faced with a difficulty, he will immediately declare it to be impossible and prepare to storm off, finally embracing the solution after half an hour of nurturing. As an Englishman I will declare the impossible to be possible and then try to find the solution.

We both get there, but by different routes. Presented with an obstacle in the shape of delays caused by human error, I will try and work it through and turn the negative into a positive. Guillaume will scream, shout, complain and generally harangue the guilty party. This can actually win some spectacular results and some impressive discounts. We do however share some common traits. We are both stubborn as mules. If he says we should move a beam from left to right, I am duty bound to suggest the opposite; after 10 minutes of arguement, one or the other will concede and suggest that we do it the other way and then we shall see what happens when it all goes wrong. I have had to swallow my words more than once, and they do taste vile.

Another difference is that working with a Frenchman, I have embraced the language and speak in French all day. Guillaume, despite running a holiday complex with numerous English clients and working with an Englishman, speaks barely a word of English. After living in France for two and a half years, I have taken on no French habits: I don't drink coffee, I have short lunch breaks, I finish work early and have no interest in food. Guillaume, on the other hand, is becoming as English as roast beef: he loves tea with milk and no sugar, prefers sandwiches to baguettes, revels in short lunch breaks and doesn't even bother with a siesta.

So, when the day is over, do we beat each other senseless? No, being opposites makes us complement each other. I deal with the big picture, he sorts out the details. He is Yin to my Yang - but don't tell him that or he'll want to be Yang.

We say Non!

It appears that graffiti does work after all. Some local joker had painted metre-high 'NON' signs all over the roads of Laguépie and it appears to do the trick.

France decided to say no to the EU constitution. This despite the fact that they sent a copy of the constitution to every person eligible to vote. My friend Guillaume showed me the two-inch thick tomes that the state had sent to him - one each for him and his wife, in case they refuse to share reading material.

I was in fact the first person to open them and try to read them. Judging from Guillaume's comments I was probably the first person in France to open one. The pages that I read seemed rather to be a statement of the bleeding obvious, with generalisations about every citizen having the right to live, the right to freedom, the right not to be tortured, the right to.... I got a little bored at this point and glazed over.

I think that the whole vote was swung by the fact that nobody really knew what it was all about, and if in doubt about something, give it the thumbs-down. There is nothing that a Frenchman likes more than turning his nose up at something, and good luck to him.

While the French have been voting with their feet, I have been wading knee-deep through woolly British ex-pats. The latest potential clients for my renovation business are really something special.

I was introduced to them by my brain-damaged electrician friend. They have a sprawling property that used to be a vineyard that has fallen on hard times - potentially rather good. The first catch is that they are teachers. Nothing against that noble profession, but woolly is truly the word for them. The second catch: the sprawling mass of buildings is owned by a syndicate - another name for a committee. There are nine of them, including five of them called John, and to make any decision they all have to agree. Since when did any teacher make a decision - let alone a committee of nine of them?

The meeting started badly with the one male not called John being late for the rendezvous. Then it went from bad to worse as he showed me the blank emptiness where he wanted me to build him a terrace - maybe out of wood, maybe out of concrete, maybe not.... did I have any ideas?

Yes, I did have an idea: get your head straight and remember what a builder is. Ours is perhaps not the oldest profession, but we operate in the same way: you tell us what you want, we do it for you and you pay us. Simple. He then suggested that we might like to have a glass of wine and talk about not very much.

The clock was ticking and I was itching to get off home. In a Herculean feat of tongue-biting I managed to stop short of speaking my mind and made off in haste. In fact, I left in such a hurry that I left my brain-damaged electrician friend behind, and for all I know he may still be there discussing the potential possibilities of navel contemplation. What I do know is that if they have a referendum on the abolition of clients, I'm voting OUI.

Under Siege

The south of France is once again under siege by the army of ill clad Northern Europeans hoping to escape from the wrath of the northern winds and to profit from our haven of peace and tranquillity.

Chez nous, is no exception. Two small words appear to have quadrupled our visitor numbers this year. The magic words are swimming pool, and these words bring all kinds of people scuttling out of the dark cobwebs of your past and smack-bang into your present day.

Our latest visitors have turned up to stay with us for a week on the pretext of having once lived in a house five doors down from us nearly 10 years ago. If that is not a flimsy connection, I don't know what is. In fairness to them I have to say that they have very diligently kept in touch with us all through our gypsy wanderings. We have had more different telephone listings than you can find in the Yellow Pages and a veritable A-Z of addresses. Patience pays off, and they are profiting from the southern sun. They used to be a wonderfully quiet and peaceful couple, but have recently had two volume-increasing additions.

Our home is generally a Mecca of calm and silence. The sound of a cat's sinews moving inside its skin when it stretches after yet another

10-hour sleep, is one of the noisiest events of our day. I have also asked the cows in the backfield to chew their cud a little more quietly from time to time. Two small children, one at about a metre high and the other at about two-thirds of that, are a somewhat rude awakening, in more ways than one; the volume of noise that they create is way out of proportion to their size.

It is of course a great joy to meet old friends once again and always fun to rediscover each other's foibles. This particular couple take being laid-back to the extreme, to the point of being horizontal. Last weekend we took them to the town of Najac in the Aveyron valley. This place is breathtakingly splendid: a huge semi-ruined castle dominates a medieval slate-roofed town perched on steep hillsides surrounded by thickly wooded gorges.

I'm sure that you get the picture - it is truly incredible. Did it provoke a reaction? Did it hell. I had to wring a reaction out of them, and when my suggestion that perhaps we might all like to go and visit the fine castle was met by a universal 'I don't mind..... not bothered' kind of reaction, that was the final straw.

I marshalled the reluctant tourists into the castle, read the guide book out loud cover to cover, bombarded them with facts and enthusiasm and I have to say that I was rewarded by their enjoyment. The small children were somewhat less than impressed by the difference between merlins and crenelles and the methods of siege warfare, but did seem to enjoy climbing onto the battlements and looking over the sheer drops to the river below, just stopping short of taking a fast short trip to meet it.

Some people wear their hearts on their sleeves and others take a little more work, but as I said to them at the end of the day, you all really enjoyed yourselves and it is all thanks to Trev. I love a challenge.

Under Pressure

All things come to an end, and building projects either coast pleasantly to an end or scream to a halt, I am currently experiencing the latter. I was given a completely derelict barn less than three months ago and asked to create a four bedroom, two bathroom home. This is no mean feat when you consider that it was a three-sided cattle shed with a busted roof, I have had to build up the fourth side and in the remaining three sides I have had to punch numerous door and window openings and line them with cut stone.

Myself and my trusty colleague Guillaume have done almost all of the work ourselves but decided to contract out the tricky split-level first-floor carpentry. This was probably a good idea because I have seen carpenters brought to tears when they watch me hacking at a stone with a wood chisel; it is not really my medium.

We were quite happy with our choice of carpenter until he eventually turned up nearly three weeks late, not late by French standards but hellishly late for my schedule.

For some reason the clients have got it into their heads that I can do all the work in three months. Despite the fact that I never said that I could, the deadline for the end of June appears to have stuck.

I managed to stop just short of hugging the carpenter when he turned up, just as well because he had a face like thunder, he turned up with a lorry full of timber and enough noisy power tools to drown out the London Symphony Orchestra.

He was possessed by the somewhat anti-social habit of starting work, and his chainsaw, at six in the morning - rather to the disgruntlement of Guillaume and his chambres d'hôtes next door.

Nevertheless, in a few short days he managed to transform one huge pile of timber into two piles, one pile of thin timber and a mountain of chippings and sawdust. Despite never sweeping up his mess he succeeded in making a first class job of the floor and I was compelled to admit that I was marginally impressed.

All of this has opened the floodgates for us, the plumber and our brain-damaged electrician. As fast as I can put partition walls up, the electrician comes over to me and says that he has forgotten to run yet another cable, so the wall comes down and then back up again, but the overall motion is forwards. It damned well needs to be because the kitchen fitters are in next Monday. This Monday there was not a single wall in the kitchen area, but we have nearly rectified that situation.

The lack of French doors in the kitchen area is close to being remedied. The first time that they arrived on site the frames and windows were a mere four centimetres too large. Probably better too big than too small, but nonetheless they had to be returned and cut down to size. I must have thought 'never again' at least a dozen times this last week and promptly forgot it when I received a phone call asking me to take on another project in the autumn to take me through the winter. Did I turn it down? Hell, no, I love the punishment.

Moi Tarzan

I had a little bit of a Tarzan moment the other day. The reason for my chest beating, leopard skin leotard moment was yet another uninvited guest to the garden bountiful.

As I may have mentioned once or twice (or perhaps a dozen times), the rural south west of France is positively teeming with wildlife; if it is not Bambis bouncing off your bonnet in the mist, it is hares zigzagging down the road in front of your headlights.

Our garden in particular appears to have big signs all around it welcoming all comers. Some of them are fairly benign: frogs with stripes, toads in the swimming pool and a famous he/she cat called Simon/Simone. Some of them are just plain unlucky, such as the mole who has taken up residence. I know he is there because he keeps chucking up the odd lump of soil; this is quite a feat in itself because the house is built on solid rock and there is not much more than a couple of inches of soil in the best places.

I do feel sorry for poor old Mr Mole, or Monsier Taupe as the French would call him. I'm sure that he must be the saddest of all moles, ruing the day he made his geographical choice whilst applying yet another band aid to his rock-damaged head.

Others are a little more unpleasant - such as our latest visitor, who chose a beautiful sunny afternoon to make his appearance.

We were sat by the pool (I just thought that I would get that one in to inspire a bit of jealousy), reading, snoozing, all those sort of Sunday afternoon things, when I heard a vicious hiss and the tinkle of a bell. I knew what the bell was: one of our cats. The bells are designed to scare off birds (go back to the drawing board Mr collar designer) but the hissing was a sound that I had never heard before.

I ran over to investigate and was confronted by the sight of Calypso, the black and white cat, locked into battle with an enormous snake, green and yellow and a good metre long.

Faced with fight or flight, I made the wrong decision and waded in. For some obscure reason I was more scared for the cat than anything else and managed to push her aside.

This was followed by a somewhat bizarre chase along the wall that runs the length of the pool. (These things can really move fast.) His Nemesis came in the shape of a fairly large rock that I hoisted above my head and let fly in his direction.

His death throes gave me time for a little post mortem, and I pretty firmly established that I had dispatched a non-venomous grass snake, the sort of thing that would give you a nasty suck. How was I to know that while I was getting all primordial and in touch with my inner caveman?

Les Gangsters

Those damned uninvited guests just keep on coming. A more cynical person might pose the question, 'What exactly made you choose to visit the swimming pool-owning couple in the south of France this summer, rather than last year when they were frying in a gîte without a stick of shade?'

The latest freeloaders turned up on the pretext that one of them once shared a student house with Sue over 20 years ago - a slim connection I know, but good enough to blag a weekend jolly.

In fairness, I have to grudgingly admit that they were excellent company and even helped with the cooking, and they did bring the visitor bonus. The visitor bonus is not a monetary or material benefit, although both are welcome. It comes in the shape of a gentle shove to knock us out of our usual routine and get us out and about. Last Saturday was the occasion of the great Caylus rock festival, a close rival to Glastonbury but without the rain, the fields, the crowds and the bands. In fact, it was one small band doing covers of classic rock tracks and a handful of people in the village square.

We have finally become wise to the French way of going to an evening concert. When we first got here we brought our English ways with us, we rushed down an evening meal and got to the venue at about 7.30, only to be greeted by an empty venue, being obliged to knock back endless beers through boredom and heading off home before anything seemed to happen.

We got it right this time, we went with our guests to a riverside restaurant, ate, drank and made merry and finally rolled up at the venue after 11 o'clock. By this time, the furnace heat of the day had cooled down and Caylus was starting to rock.

The music, being mainly old rock covers, perfectly suited a bunch of over-40 ageing rockers (except me, who is only 39). It led to the usual game of guessing the intro, much to the shame of Eddie, our visitor, who guessed the Status Quo track in the first two of the 12 bars.

In a somewhat bizarre twist of events, I happened to mention my strained Achilles tendon and was promptly offered treatment by an archaeologist with healing powers.

Despite being an archaeologist, he didn't appear to have a beard with small creatures living in it, so I decided to give him a go. It was a bit strange to have my ankle stroked by a fellow male in a public place, but it did the trick. It gave us the opportunity for a bit of a chat and he pointed out a couple of the local Brit characters, such as the Zimbabwean sanctions-busting smuggler with his sidekick, locally known as the baby-faced gangster - one with a price on his head, as rumour has it.

Who would have thought it from a Saturday night in rural France - rock music, healing and gangsters? Keep those freeloading tourists rolling. I wonder if that bloke I sat next to on a bus once fancies a holiday?

Kicking the Blues

I had to call in my old friend Pat the melancholy plumber last weekend. He has earned that title partly from being called Patrice and being a plumber, but mostly from permanently having a face longer than a French unemployment queue.

The occasion of his being summoned was the unfortunate state of the sand filter on our swimming pool pump. The whole thing needed changing and, as a builder, I am expressly forbidden from touching any of those plastic things that carry water or electricity.

I have touched them several times in the past and the results usually involve people being hurled across the room, plunged into darkness or drowned under floods of water.

Pat turned up bright and early on the Saturday morning. There was something strange about him. He gratefully accepted his cup of tea and started rolling his first cigarette, but something was missing.

Normally the first thing that he does is to open his heart to all the woes that are his lot, and these have been many of late. In fact he has been the dictionary definition of melancholia for quite some time.

His case is not a particularly rare ailment out here, his marriage having recently fallen victim to a house renovation. He is French by birth but had spent most of his adult life in Croydon, before hearing the call of his native homeland. He and his family relocated to France to pursue the dream of renovating a sprawling place in the French countryside. All of the circumstances were textbook. He would spend all day out at work, plumbing for a living, then get his tools out in the evenings and weekends to create the dream home for his family, his wife meanwhile reminding him about not having proper kitchen and bathroom facilities.

Rooms got half done, more reminders, creeping resentment, fatigue, complaints about not enough time spent with family, more fatigue, less getting done for more effort, arguments, wife falls into arms of another man... melancholia.

He did drop to the bottom of the pit, and it is not a nice thing to see your friends in a bad way. We tried to support him but there never seemed to be any way to get that sad look out of his eyes.

On this Saturday morning he seemed to have gained something. He had sparkle in his eyes and a spring in his step. He had found a girlfriend.

I said: "Good for you". This was not enough for Sue, who wanted to know about the girl's age, about her parents, where she lived and all those other unnecessary details.

The important thing was that we got all of the necessary plumbing done with barely a swear word and no grumbles at all.

We finished the day with light hearts, glad to see that things had worked out for a good friend, helped by a glowing feeling of justification that we had been right to say that things would turn out okay.

He now swears that he will never do another renovation. My business is renovation so what does that make me, a masochist?

Paris, Set and Match

My world fell apart last weekend. First I discovered that George VI was dead, then I found out that Einstein had followed him, the war in Vietnam was not going well for the French colonial forces and Grace Kelly was living it up on the Riviera.

The reason for my being au courant with not-quite-so-current affairs was a huge stack of back copies of the magazine Paris Match from the 1950s and 60s that we picked at a brocante or flea market that was held in our local town. The French brocantes have much in common with their English cousins: the same old tat trawled out on several stalls.... coffee grinders and cleaned-up old tools with price tags that keep your jaw firmly glued to the ground.

It was a Sunday, I was short of reading material as usual. Somebody trying to sell old magazines and I had a few centimes in my pocket so it was, wait for it, a Paris Match made in heaven. My euphoria at picking up the whole box for just 10 euros soon turned to dismay as I lugged the hundredweight of elderly paper through the 30-degree midday heat back to the car.

After sweating off 50 per cent of my body mass we found our way back home and settled down on the terrace with a cup of tea and a world of forgotten news at our fingertips.

In a lot of ways it was surprising to see just how little had changed. Paris Match was the forerunner of magazines such as Hello; it featured pictures of Barbara Stanwyck getting out of her limousine and a surprisingly heavy dose of articles about the British royals. I suppose other people's aristocrats are quite a novelty when you don't have any of your own, on account of having separated their heads from their bodies.

The adverts are often the most revealing about the times. There was a heavy presence of vacuum cleaners and cigarettes, and a fridge with a built-in radio. I don't know why that didn't catch on. The thing that struck me most was not how far we had moved on, but how these days we seem to have stopped looking forwards. Many were the adverts for nylon that declared that the days of ironing shirts were numbered and that you could even buy trousers that would never need to be pressed.

What did we do with this invention? Consigned it to the bin because we didn't like electrostatic charges and rashes when we sweated. Progress comes at a price, you know.

Technology seemed so much more exciting 40 years ago. Everybody was talking about helicopters, Valerie Giscard D'Estaing was taking a flight on the first Concorde and there were huge adverts for the hovercraft that could get you across the channel in half an hour.

We scrapped the Concordes in favour of 747s with a design that predates manned flight. We dumped hovercraft because they vibrated and instead of all having our own personal helicopters we just keep one communal one as an ambulance.

There was one bit of good news: it looked as if the Common Market was going to be a big success; they might even ratify the constitution one day.

Kitten Hell

Events in the tale of woe that purports to be the life of Trevor have just taken a turn for the worse.

I thought I was just about managing to hold my own at fifth place in Sue's affections. I have long since given up trying to improve on my position, I just can't compete with those darned cats. I did think that I was doing a valiant job of holding off the stray Siamese called Simon - a bit manky, a bit aggressive and not house-trained. I did think that I could at least stand up against that.

That was until he pulled out his hidden ace. He went and got himself pregnant. Quite a feat, one that I stand no chance of emulating, even if I wanted to.

This immediately entitled him/her to extra privilges: extra meals and gentle cooing. It would even have led to caresses if he/she would have allowed it. As pregnancies do, it has led to the inevitable conclusion: there are now four kittens.

For a while it seemed as if they may not have survived, or that perhaps the farmer may have dispatched them in farmer's normal pragmatic way. But Sue spotted four big-eyed, big-eared, cute little bundles scampering around the bushes in a field near the house.

Sue's eyes lit up and my heart sank correspondingly. This did not have the makings of a move down the pecking order, it was looking more like full-scale relegation down to the Ace Double Glazing Retired Workers League that only plays one Sunday per month.

Unfortunately for Sue, the kittens were by this stage about eight weeks old and had never even been close to a human being. They were not particularly happy about meeting one. Sue has countered this by moving into full David Attenborough making-friends-with-a-woop-of-gorillas mode; she has put down food and water and can be seen at dawn and dusk talking softly to a bush that she claims is full of kittens.

The other night when I went outside to find her, all I could see was someone with a plastic fishing rod and a woolly mouse on the end of it fishing. All became clear when I saw a big pair of eyes chasing the mouse.

I must admit that I did lack the patience to hang around and see exactly what might unfold, but then Sue, tapping on the patio doors dripping with blood and with a cat basket in her hand, told me that she had reached her goal.

It looks as if we have got another grey cat to add to the menagerie (we have already got one that she rescued from beneath a car). There is yet another grey one to be caught and then a black one and then a black and white one. Knowing her determination it seems likely that they will all eventually succumb. And she was further spurred in her efforts by the mad old lady next door saying that she was going to tell the farmer where they were so that he could shoot them. I narrowly prevented the old lady from being euthanised on the spot.

My position gets worse. Maybe I should try looking cute and playing with a ball of wool. Tough competition, but I won't give up without a fight.

Quel Scorcher

The mercury has stopped rising. That doesn't mean that summer has been halted, it means that the mercury can't move anymore because it has reached the top and had to stop.

Every day starts the same: clear blue skies and a pleasantly warm sun which then develops a personality disorder and becomes a psychopathic baby-eating, axe-wielding, tourist-burning dervish. The sun is refusing to give way to that cooling solution that we used to know intimately as rain. Rain is something that we have become strangers to; we are living in the land of the dessicated.

The scalding sun that rarely ever lets the temperature drop below 30 and has burnt the lush green countryside into a uniform Desert Rat khaki does have certain fringe benefits, not least of which is that Sue and countless hordes of young beauties have decided that clothes are no longer for them and that anything more than a small piece of string is just too hot to wear.

This upside is of course accompanied by a downside: moutons dressed as lambs are also shedding vestments at a dangerous rate. I do think that the gendarmes should be given certain powers to cover up the more atrocious sights, especially those amongst the whiter tourist fraternity.

On second thoughts, there is not really much point in giving the gendarmes any powers at all because most of them are asleep under the shade of a tree as they slow down ready for the great August annual stopping of the world from turning ceremony - or month's holiday, as some would call it.

The other bonus to come from this overheating is that it kills plants off at a scary rate. Horticulturists might not like this sentiment, but when at times you have lost your wife in the grass surrounding your house you are only too glad when something comes along to kill it off. Where I once spent days hacking back a wilderness in which great thistles reigned supreme, there is only dust.

The cats are none too impressed by the heat. Shedding a few pounds and having a haircut would probably help them, but in the absence of the willpower to go on a diet they have taken to splaying themselves on the tiled floors and trying to suck out the subterranean cool. In fact, they are looking rather like a tiger skin rug that we saw in a chateau we were visiting the other day. It was lying there quite unhappily, with his head still attached to his skin, as was once the fashion, until a passing tourist caught his espadrille in its mouth and gave us a much-appreciated comedy moment. It just goes to show you that even dead animals can get a bit of revenge on you when you least expect it.

What can I expect from tomorrow? More concrete-setting, lawn-killing sun. If it gets too hot to work, what can be done? Follow those gendarmes: sit under a tree and dream of holidays.

Spot the Mitty

A funny thing happens to Brits when you take them out of their natural surroundings and dump them into a foreign country (besides them turning a queer shade of shrimp pink if the temperature rises above the 20-degree level). It is a strange kind of metamorphosis that takes place when they forsake their predictable former existence for something rather different.

The changes that overtake them are sometimes driven by economic necessity - a bit ironic perhaps, when many of your average aspiring Brits have managed to raise enough cash to buy themselves a pile in France that is 33 times larger than the semi-detached rabbit hutch they used to inhabit in the UK. Unfortunately, the project often turns out to swallow their life's savings and they are then obliged to spend their retirement dream earning a living.

This can pose something of a challenge if, for instance, you have made your living being a development engineer for an electrical transducer concern. You may find your skills not readily transferable. And so people start working in fields that they have no experience nor knowledge of. I have met a former British Airways baggage handler who has set himself up as a master builder and is doing a roaring trade. There is not much baggage to handle in rural France, but plenty of houses to be done up and people to be done over.

Another favourite refuge is estate agency. Most people have lived in a house and possibly bought and sold once or twice. This counts as instant qualification, and with agency fees running at anything up to 10 per cent, who wouldn't be tempted? I know of at least one secretary, a former pub landlord and a nature documentary producer who have reinvented themselves as the ideal persons to advise you about the most important investment of your life. You may even have read articles written by them in French Property News.

This is the fun part about moving abroad. Not only do you dump all your old mates who knew you when you were digging trenches for a fiver an hour (in my case, laying blocks), you can also keep those embarrassing family members away from your social circle as they are only with you for a few days a year. This can avoid them saying things like "I used to tell Graham (now known more suavely as Gilles) that telesales is no way for a grown man to make a living".

Some people don't need the money as much as they need the status. We know one girl who didn't even finish her YTS course in a works canteen who, since she married somebody with enough cash to be sure that she never needs to work, has re-invented herself as a cordon bleu chef and has even blagged as far as catering a parties for some rather well-known names of English politics and media.

The worst culprit of all? A hairy-arsed Dorset brickie who runs a renovation enterprise who was introduced at a party as a freelance journalist. Did he go on to reveal to anyone that the closest he has ever got to The Times was when he delivered it as paperboy? Did he hell. He blagged it, the same as everybody else.

Fuming

You have to admire the dedication of certain nations. The Italians have always been dedicated to flair and style, the Germans to invading neighbouring countries, the Dutch to pornography and drugs.

The French are dedicated to the long lunch break, the drinking of wine, the religious avoidance of strenuous activity and anything longer than a 35-hour week. None of these, though, even come close to their stubborn dedication to the art of smoking, which they continue to pursue with a vengeance despite the global ground swell against it.

Ostensibly, France is alongside its European neighbours when it comes to legislation. They are all there: the rules about not smoking in restaurants, public places and all that malarkey. Do the French observe these rules? Well, ask the woman selling fruit and veg with a fag in her hand; I suggest that the answer will be no. Not only do the French smoke against rules, they also smoke in contravention of common sense.

The other day I saw one man smoking whilst riding his moped and a lady in a restaurant with a fork in one hand and a cigarette in the other.

The best of all was a smoking jogger. I don't know quite what his reasoning was; perhaps the jogging was a way of pumping the nicotine around his body a little more efficiently.

Whatever you think about smoking (I'm fairly ambivalent, having given up my one-pack-a-week habit some years ago) you have to admit that the French can do it with style. I don't know quite how, but young French women somehow manage to make it look sexy in a way that their English cousins never could. It is something to do with a self-confidence and a belief that they look cool, and to hell with the rest.

Sue struggles a bit with the prevalence of cigarettes, having kicked her addiction a couple of years ago, transforming herself into a born-again non-smoker. She now has to wash her hair if she sits next to somebody in the cinema who has smoked in the last hour. You can imagine her nightmare when she goes into a café, where you have to practically cut your way through the smoke with a knife to get in, and that is just on the terrace.

The worst place to be for an anti-smoker is anywhere where there are teenagers. All the teenagers smoke. They all chew gum and they all smoke. I believe it is in the school rules that they have to.

When the teenagers grow up, if they go into any type of profession that involves manual work they will continue to smoke. Absolutely all builders, gardeners and mechanics do so.

Mind you, even the doctors smoke in their surgeries. And the interesting thing: they grow up into old men that sit around together on park benches and smoke. The rest of the world tells them that smoking shortens your life, but I'm not sure about the evidence.

I think that dedication to your cause pays off. I could maybe handle taking up smoking again, but I'm not sure that I could manage the jogging.

French Exchange

It's August. As inexorably as the sun rises, the world round here slows down. The French state sends out demands for more money, so the marriages and relations of British ex-pats hit the skids.

We have seen countless couples who thought that a life in the sun would mean an end to all their troubles. All it really means is that your problems are better-tanned and a little harder to focus on through an alcoholic fug. Things seemed to be getting desperate when even the gay couples that we know started to fall apart. Then news started to come through of a brave new world that was coming into being at a village we shall call Valhalla.

Valhalla is a rather scary village in the centre of the forest. As these places tend to be, it was a sleepy place where the locals married each other, counted their livestock on their numerous surplus digits and lived simply.

Things were all very well until the Great War took away all those close relatives that you needed for marrying and looking after you in your old age.

The place became deserted and fell into a steep decline until the hippies discovered it in the 1960s, set up a goat farm, breathed new life into the place and set about creating a multi-national Hippiedom. This Valhalla has since become home to many of the new wave of Brit middle-class asylum seekers, with all their associated baggage. The hippie lifestyle spoke of many things, most of them centred around drugs and music, but one of the central tenets was free love and all that.

There were all kinds of things going on in Valhalla already. When the local electrician got on rather too well with his neighbour's wife, he managed, in the end, to make a successful trade for his old one. These practices have left a mark on the local psyche, and when the new wave hit town and hit problems they were able to turn to old solutions.

A, was married to B, a new found pillar of the community, drank too much, got bored and tried out several of the locals, and B got his own back with his students. Several children resulted, and presumably they at least they knew who the mother was. C and D moved in, several more kids in tow. A got friendly with D... you can guess the rest: a neat and practical solution to splitting up with your current partner. None of that speed dating nonsense - you can't get much speedier than nipping next door. And once you scratch the surface of this having an affair business you find out that nearly everybody you know is having one, had one, or thinking seriously about getting one before it's too late.

Personally speaking, faced with some of these ex-pats, if I were at one of these wife-swapping orgies where you throw your car keys in, I think I would take the car instead, even if it was an old 2CV with four flat tyres.

Le Deluge

If you have been reading and hearing about the terrible drought and water shortages that are hitting the south west of France, don't believe a single word of it.

We have got metres of water. In fact, I literally had water coming out of my ears a couple of days ago.

We had the whole summer delivery of rain arrive in the space of one afternoon. It went from sunshine to thunderstorm to deluge in one fell swoop.

The first few drops were very welcome. No more need to top up the swimming pool, good for the garden and all that malarkey. Then it became apparent that it was not going to be any old storm coming our way. The eclipse-style black sky was the giveaway.

You would have thought that living nearly at the top of a hill would be a good guarantee of not being flooded. Think again. The previous owner put some French doors in the wall that holds back the water that runs off the field behind us, and to make extra sure that they would be tested to the maximum he built a wall against the corner of the house to stop any water from escaping down the hill.

After a couple of small warning floods, I had made moves to redress the balance by blocking up the French doors and breaking away some of the concrete that he had installed. Too little, and not soon enough. It was when the rain started to climb towards the second course of blockwork that I started to worry. Gutters started to overflow and the level just kept rising. It was starting to seep into the house, a foretaste of things to come. Faced with adversity, there were just two possibilities, break out the beer and say to hell with it all, or get the buckets out. Somebody had padlocked the fridge and so buckets it was.

I started bailing like a boiler stoker on the Titanic, but the faster I bailed the harder it rained. Sue had to unglue her nose from the pane of glass that she had been watching me through and pitch in. We bailed and we bailed to no avail. At this point Sue looked towards the fishpond which is conveniently sited a little higher up the garden. Goldfish were starting to make a bid for freedom.

At this point I reached (wait for it) saturation point, I was soaked through to my pants and beyond. Everything was squelching. We were making no impact and the rain was getting harder. Desperate times and all that. You sometimes have to stand back from the immediate problem and look at the bigger picture. I ripped the drainpipe off the wall and frantically clawed through the soil and rock to expose the drainage pipes, and pulled them apart. Eureka - the level began to stabilise and after a while actually began to fall.

I thought that we had had a hard time of it until I drove past a neighbour the next day. The farmer had recently ploughed the field just above his house and now most of the field was piled up against his front door.

From now on, the only water I want to see is fermented water in a green bottle with the word 'beer' written on the label.

Autumn 2005

Shop till you Drop

I am not one of life's natural shoppers. In fact, the very word shopping, brings me out in a full-body sweat accompanied by uncontrollable tremors.

In my ideal world each shop would contain just one item: the one that you need. It would have at least one cashier for every client and maybe a bar in the corner for those days when you wanted to linger and browse a little.

In some of these ways, France is the answer to a lot of my prayers. You are not troubled, for instance, by bothersome choices such as whether or not to buy the Chilean, Antipodean or Eastern European Sauvignon. Buy the French one or nothing. France is still run as a protectionist economy. Despite anything you may have heard about it being a member of the EU (they only say that to annoy the English), France doesn't actually participate in any type of Common Market. If it is not produced in France at the cost of vast subsidies, or else imported from somewhere that has a particularly cosy trade agreement, you can forget buying it. It doesn't matter if it is cheaper, better or more popular, you can't have it.

This does make some kinds of shopping bewilderingly easy. There is not, for example, that much choice in the way of cheeses. Each division such as bries, camemberts etc has lots of different regional choices but there are only the basic few choices: white, blue or yellow. The same goes for wine. There are dozens of Gaillac reds, but if you don't like Gaillac red you are going to go thirsty.

This is all fantastic news for me, on those rare occasions that Sue can hoodwink me into a trip to the supermarket. The trip is a doddle: cheese aisle, blue; wine aisle, green bottle containing red; bread aisle, thin or fat stick depending on level of hunger.

There are other hidden advantages to the Saturday shop fest. If you don't get up too early you can hit the shops just before noon. On the dot of 11.45 the shop assistants start to get anxious and irritable, by 11.55 they are fiddling with the shutters and by 12.00 it is hard to believe that any shops were ever open - on the high street there is just tumbleweed and a few people clutching baguettes and riding mopeds. This unfortunately means that you have no other recourse but to retire to a café or restaurant for the next couple of hours. If this visit should include a nicely-chilled bottle of rosé, the chances of finding the motivation to look around one of those sales emporiums are slim.

This brings me to the other good thing about France. The sales staff generally outnumber the customers - not because there are a lot of sales staff, it is just that there are not many people buying things.

People just don't buy much here. It is not like the UK where the high streets are full of people laden down like packhorses with their bargains. They buy little and not very often. I like that philosophy. In fact, I have just talked myself into a 180-degree turn, I love shopping, but only in France, just before midday, when I don't need anything.

Stop

The normally sleepy backwater that we inhabit has just taken a sharp turn towards the catatonic. The atmostphere in this house is making a snail conference seem like rather a frantic affair.

The reasons for this are twofold. I have just stopped work for my annual holiday (something of a misnomer as it is the first one since arriving here nearly three years ago), and a couple of friends have arrived for their two-week holiday.

This combination of events and people can only really lead to catastrophe. Individually we are all highly motivated, self-employed, or professional people. Unfortunately, when we stop work and meet up for a holiday, all motivation gets itself motivated out of the window, and all physical abilities leave, to be replaced by back-up systems of minimum life support. We once went on holiday to Crete together. At least we believe it was Crete; instead of our planned adventurous discovering of uncharted territory we ate, slept and dozed our way through a whole week, never venturing away from the swimming pool.

This holiday has all the hallmarks of a slow-motion action replay of Crete. They turned up on the Saturday, having driven through the night; this necessitated a large lunch, followed by a small snooze, and thus the die was cast. The pile of guide books and leaflets of interesting things to see and do is gathering dust in the corner. The pile of unused teabags is slowly going down as a dice is lazily rolled to see whose turn it is to put the kettle on; the pile of empty bottles is growing alarmingly, and if we continue to consume the fresh produce at the present rate, we may have to resort to minor acts of cannibalism if a tiring trip down the hill to the shop is to be avoided.

Even the cats have caught the mood - the older ones have all found bushes to sleep under until it is time to wake up and go to bed. Louis the little kitten manages to push his toy mouse about a little bit before nodding off.

We have in fact managed to talk about activities. A canoeing trip down the Aveyron valley has been discussed - we have imagined the rapids, the dramatic limestone cliff faces with oak trees gripping impossibly to their sides. This is as far as it has got, and likely to go. In an effort to pull ourselves out of this torpor we have booked ourselves three nights in a hotel in Biarritz, I have a sneaking suspicion that we will just be exporting our laziness to the coast, but at least we shall be able to look at the sea and imagine how it would be to walk barefoot along the beach and swim in the waves.

In fact, I can just about imagine myself there - without the effort of getting in the car and going there. Put an old Beach Boys CD and away we go.

Perhaps it will all change next week. We'll go bungee jumping and sky diving if we can just tear ourselves away from the quiet scenery, the tranquillity, the peacefulness, the hush......

Beach Ballet

After nearly two years of being land-locked away in our little rural cocoon we finally managed to break out and profit from the immense coastline that France has to offer.

Our easiest destination would have been the Med, but not being the kind of people to take the easy option, we prefer the Atlantic coast. This is not just because the Atlantic coast is less popular and therefore less spoilt, it is mainly because of the awesome splendour of the Atlantic crashing against the European continent. There are miles and miles of silver sand beaches with hundreds of surfers bobbing in the swells like seals in testament to the power of the waves.

We headed for Biarritz. It has echoes of Bournemouth, a town first proposed in a more elegant time, later further developed but retaining a certain charm.

In fact, I hate to admit it, but the French manage to maintain a stylish resort without ever stooping to the gimcrack, souvenir shop, kiss-me-quick shabbiness that is the scourge of English resorts. This despite the propensity of the surf shops and VW camper vans that the coast is attacked by.

We installed ourselves in our luxury hotel. We were lucky enough to have a postage stamp bed, a sea glimpse across the dual carriageway and a balcony the size and shape of a B52 gun turret.

We could breakfast on this balcony one at a time, if we remained standing and tossed croissants through an open door, but it was cheap and available.

Availability was no small factor as we had chosen the time of the festival of culture and music for our visit. What better place for your hard-working British builder to enjoy a spot of R&R than in a sophisticated, upmarket town of culture!

The presence of culture manifested itself as we sat upon the beach, dozing in the sunshine, watching the waves and wondering what the huge scaffolding stage sandwiched between us and the ocean was there for. A burst of classical music heralded the entrance of one heavily muscled and some other scantily-clad waif-like dancers on the stage.

This was ballet, happening before our very eyes. I had never seen a ballet, nor ever wanted to see one. But it was there in front of me, free of charge, and I have to say that I found myself enthralled.

It is one of the benefits of living in a socialist country that such frivolities as the arts are heavily subsidised and made available to the masses. I was actually glad of every Euro that I give to the French state as I enjoyed a sublime hour-and-a-half of dancers straining every sinew against a backdrop of cliffs and crashing waves, quite extraordinary.

It made me feel that perhaps I could have been a dancer. All that I lacked was the strength, poise, balance, agility, sense of rhythm and stamina. Oh well, in the next life maybe. In the meantime, I'll stick to the building work.

Swallows and Kittens

It is coming close to that time when we have to face up to reality and accept that maybe summer is beginning to draw to a close.

It is now approaching the last week in September and our huge colony of hirondelles or swallows have packed up their suitcases and vacated our garage. Much as I loved to see the little fellows flying in and out of our garage and gambolling in the summer skies, they have left behind them rather more than fond memories.

There were at least half-a-dozen nests in the rafters and most of them played host to more than one hatching. The consequence of this has been large piles of guano, all over every single tool that I own.

This does of course have negative impacts for the more squeamish builder, but also offers some fringe benefits. My brain-damaged electrician friend has ceased to ask to borrow anything and has gone out and bought his own tools.

The biggest problem is that the job that we managed to keep postponing on account of swallow privacy laws, ie, the great garage clean-up, has now manifested itself.

This wouldn't really appear to be too daunting a task. We moved out of our two-bedroom apartment in Dorchester three years ago with all of our worldly goods in a transit van and the cats in my Escort van. We are now living in a four-bedroom house with three garages (the swallow garage being the only one not full of rubble or scaffolding). The house appears to be full, so that must mean that there is next to nothing in the garage.

Not so. I appear to have gone from being a one-man band who can fit all of his tools in an Escort to being a one-man band who needs an articulated lorry to move his scaffolding, generators, power tools, kitchen sinks etc.

We have gone from an apartment where the gardeners take care of everything, to having to do such menial tasks ourselves, necessitating the ownership of mowers, strimmers, jet washers, tools, tools and more tools.

It was no good looking at it, we just had to lug it all out so we could start the clean-up. In true fashion the rain came just as we got it all outside, but at least we were helped by little Louis. Louis is the feral cat that Sue recently rescued and tamed. He spent the first six weeks in hiding from us beneath a chair, but has now come out of the closet to take his rightful place in the family home.

In some bizarre way Louis is omnipresent. If you move a box, he is in it, look on a shelf, he is there, move something outside and he is between your feet, making you fall flat on your face.

When you finally recover from your concussion and look up, he is in the tree above you, looking down. In spite of Louis' help, we managed to clear up all the guano, desiccated mice and dead bats, and restored some sort of order for another year. Roll on global warming - if they never leave, surely we'll never have to clean.

Avocat Dip

Some things begin wrong, some achieve wrongness. Others have 'wrong' written all the way through them like a stick of rock.

Such was the decision taken by my dear friend and colleague Guillaume last year.

Being the owner of a substantial holiday complex, he found himself in the common position of being property-rich and cash-poor. After paying back his loans he found himself short of funds and desperate to unlock some cash.

The answer to all his dreams took the shape of the barn at the end of his drive and nearly next to his house. It needed renovating, he didn't have the money to do it himself, so why not sell it and make some money? Even better, why not sell it to his in-laws?

There is a point, when offering advice, that you just have to give up, let go and see what happens. The feeling of watching a friend make a bad decision is rather like being a bystander during a car crash. You want to help, you want to make it not happen, but you have to let the inevitable take its course.

Things started well. They were all the best of friends, I was doing the renovation on the barn, cheques were flying backwards and forwards, everything was rosy. They were on course to move in on the proposed date.

One of the last jobs to be done was the installation of the septic tank. It was problematic finding a suitable spot for the huge concrete monolith. Guillaume jumped in with a solution. "Put it on my land," he said. Oh, how those words haunt me.

Things unfortunately started to go pear-shaped and relations started to sour. Cheques became later and eventually dried up altogether; neighbourly disputes broke out about washing, swimming pools, patio furniture. You get the picture. Communications halted, except in the form of registered letters sent via the post office.

When bullets are flying, there is always somebody caught in the crossfire. The first I knew about my shrapnel injury was a registered letter that dropped through my letterbox. The letter from an avocat (solicitor) told me in no uncertain terms that I had erroneously installed a septic tank on a neighbour's land and suggested that I remove it and re-site it - an operation which would cost me several thousand Euros.

In order to limit my injury to a light flesh wound, I have had to take up weapons, in the form of my own avocat, a fresh-faced youth with an office handily placed next to the Palais de Justice and hospital. He studied the paperwork, declared it to be nonsense and has now begun my noble defence.

My people will speak to their people, but not the other ones. They won't talk to each other. I might talk to some of them, but not the ones who owe me money. I won't move the tank, unless they make me. They won't fence the swimming pool, they won't take down the 10-foot fence recently erected between them.

My head hurts and they aren't even my neighbours. One good thing: at least I am not related to any of them.

Neighbours

Neighbours, everybody needs good neighbours...... good neighbours become good friends.

Whoever wrote that one probably lived on a solitary ranch in the middle of the desert. He certainly didn't live next door to one neighbour that I heard tell of recently.

A chap was quite innocently having problems with his pool alarm going off intermittently. This is a not infrequent problem as all pools in France are required to be surrounded by a childproof fence, or else be alarmed, or equipped with anti-tank devices, watchtowers and slavering rottweilers. Alarms are cheapest and therefore most popular. The pool alarm problem was not so much of a problem for the owner (who was frequently away) as for his neighbours. One slightly miffed neighbour, losing out on his beauty sleep one time too many, wound his way across to his neighbours' pool, dragged the offending item from its watery cocoon, sized it up for the quantity of grief that it conveyed against its monetary value and gave it both barrels from his shotgun before dropping it on the poor chap's doorstep.

Slightly less messy than a horse's head in the bed, but the message was just as clear.

Sometimes neighbours just take hospitality and goodwill as a given. An English roofer friend of mine has French neighbours who have decided to integrate themselves with their new Anglo-Saxon neighbours. This runs beyond the demand for beer whenever they cross the threshold; they often drop the kids off in the house, say a quick hello, explain that they will probably be back before dark, unless they are having too good a time, and go off for the day, leaving the somewhat surprised English couple to look after a menagerie of children ranging from babies to teenagers to feed and entertain for the day.

They have, on occasion, even left elderly relatives as well.

English neighbours don't generally have this reputation for taking advantage. In fact, their benefits are mainly positive, especially when it comes to an almost inexhaustible supply of gossip.

One recent piece of tittle-tattle is about an English gentleman builder with a reputation for charging like a wounded rhino. His pricing structure enabled him to construct a huge chateau-style home in the village that he mostly owned.

It now appears he has done a runner - last seen heading for far-flung places with his wife and kids in tow, hotly pursued by the long arm of the French law, leaving behind a large portfolio of unfinished projects and somewhat disgruntled homeowners.

At least he had the decency to run off with his own wife. Another builder I know used to employ a neighbour on a casual labouring basis. A generous employer, he even went to the trouble of dropping him off, wherever the job was, to do a day of digging for him.

His help was left with a shovel for company in the middle of nowhere with no means of transport, and therefore no chance of accidentally finding his employer inflagrante with his wife.

One happy builder. At least he was happy until the postlady (watch out for them, they know everything out here) burst his bubble and paved the way for a mouth full of broken teeth.

Neighbours, eh? It's a hermit's life for me.

I Predict a Riot

It's a riot out here. The gendarmes are frying innocent Arab youths in electricity sub-stations, people are out on the streets protesting and there is barely an unburnt car left in Metropolitan France.

My journeys to work have been fraught with danger. I have been swerving to avoid flying debris and catching Molotov cocktails between my teeth.

Okay, a slight exaggeration: I haven't seen any rioters quite yet, although I did see a couple of old men who didn't look very happy the other day; you could almost have said that they were borderline grumpy.

I do have my ear to the ground to check on potential riots. I rely for information from my current clients, who are obliged to live in their apartment in central Toulouse while I turn their perfectly habitable house into a windowless wreck before turning it into a latter-day Blenheim Palace - if I can work out how to put it back together.

They have given me all of the latest facts, straight from the horse's mouth, so to speak. They have not seen or heard a peep, there is nothing going on. The noisiest thing is the constant ringing of their telephone, which has nearly melted with calls from anxious relatives and friends saying how worried they are - and in the more extreme cases cancelling their flights out to visit them.

The bulk of the rioting seems to be down to media frenzy, and as these things do, it has snowballed out of all proportion. We were back in the UK for a flying visit last weekend, and saw how the British media has latched on to it. This is probably down to two major interlinked factors: a traditional British dislike of the French, probably deeply rooted in jealousy (the French had Catherine Deneuve and the Eiffel Tower, while we had Diana Dors and the Post Office Tower). The second factor is good old-fashioned schadenfreude: nothing cheers us up like a misfortune befalling somebody else, especially the French.

You can literally hear the shouts of joy coming from all the Daily Mail readers across the Channel, picturing rivers of blood on the streets of France. They may well have enjoyed their little two-week holiday in France, but it certainly helps them to get through the long winter nights to think that there are others not so far away who won't be able to sleep safely in their beds tonight.

In the absence of any riots happening on my doorstep - or indeed anywhere near it - I feel bad about not doing my bit for the International media, but really, you do need to be unhappy to riot. With the best boulangerie in France on my route to work, where I stop off in the morning to buy fresh warm pain aux raisins for myself and the lads, how could I not be happy? Memo to the Minister of the Interior: let them eat pain aux raisins, and don't lose your head.

Laid Back Brits

Appearances can be deceptive... things are not always what they seem.

What seems like a great idea - upping sticks and moving to the south west of France, for instance - can turn into the worst mistake of your life. It is possible.

Likewise, our perceptions of other people can be more than just mildly inaccurate. The accepted view between the French and the English is that the Brits are uptight and rigid whilst their Gallic cousins are laid back and positively oozing joie de vivre.

I must admit that I have always bought into this illusion - or perhaps delusion would be more accurate. The longer I spend in France, the more I have come to question what I once thought that I knew.

Just this afternoon, we were having an afternoon tea break - our mixed crew of English and French workers, along with the unfortunate British owner of our latest renovation project.

We were interrupted by the arrival of his daughter and her children. She knows all of us relatively well, and Pat the no-longer-melancholy plumber better than most. As she approached the table you could almost see her mental processes working.... she was thinking to herself: shall I go through the elaborate charade and effort of kissing all of these people on both cheeks, or shall I not bother?

Decision made: dump the rest of us and just plant a smacker on Pat. And the worst of it, none of us took a blind bit of notice - we couldn't care less.

If the same thing had happened in an all French situation it would have been grounds for excommunication, a family feud, or at least a two-hour tirade with accompanying gesticulations.

As an English person buying into the relaxed southern way of doing things, you are just as likely to fall foul of stringent guidelines. Don't even contemplate drinking the wrong coloured wine with the wrong course at lunchtime. I thought that wine just came in different colours to stop it from being boring.

Likewise, riding a bicycle has its own set of rules. You cannot just hop on a bike and go for a ride wearing everyday clothes - the sole exception being if you are wearing a beret, which overrides all dress codes. If you choose to ride a bicycle you are obliged to deck yourself in the latest copycat Tour de France outfit, there is unfortunately no upper age limit to this law.

All of these are nothing compared to the strict rules governing the regularity of mealtimes. I once tried to explain to a French friend that we tend to eat when we are hungry, and if we are not, we don't bother.

I may as well have told him that I was a Martian and lived in a block of cream cheese. He didn't understand a word of what I had said.

Living amongst so many rules does make you a little bloody-minded in the end. I think I may shortly go for a cycle ride in my jeans, at lunchtime, swigging from a bottle of red wine.

Winter 2005

Scaffold Aweigh

They tell actors never to work with children and animals. Personally, I find there are times when I will happily work with anyone I can get. I have found myself temporarily alone on site, Guillaume having decided that two weeks on a beach in Mauritius is preferable to working with me. I have therefore had to rope in help as best I can. Most things to do with creating a window opening can be done solo - beating holes and building stonework, for instance. But some things are next to impossible alone, such as lifting an oak lintel into position on the first floor.

Having prepared all of the necessary elements, cut the beam and manoeuvred it into position at the base of the scaffold, pulley positioned, I called over the temporary help. The part-time help took the form of the owner (a 50-something former soft furnishing dealer) and an Irish former window dresser who was labouring on the job. I know they don't sound very promising or useful, but they are available and cheap.

All I needed was the beam in position and then they could go away and carry on with their knitting or whatever it is that soft furnishers do to dress windows. The pulley is on a kind of swinging gallows that slots on to a corner of the scaffolding. The trick is to pull from the end of the scaffolding; this way it is difficult to pull a rectangle over. If you pull from the side, you are likely to end up wearing a scaffolding necklace.

After a quick health and safety lecture, we got to work and achieved what we set out to do. The lintel fitted perfectly. I was just standing on the scaffold making a few minor adjustments to the lintel, listening to my helpers descending. Mr Soft Furnishing was accusing Mr Window Dresser of being a bit of a porker. The debate hotted up and a weighing competition was declared. In the absence of scales and the presence of rope and pulley, a solution was discovered. Each would try to lift the other off the ground and the lighter would rise. The only fly in the ointment was the lack of elbow room at the end of the scaffolding.

Unbeknownst to me, happily tapping away with hammer and level on high, they moved to the side of the scaffolding to begin the competition. My hands were firmly grasped around the freshly installed lintel when I glanced down at my feet, which were moving away from the building. Not only that; there was a widening gap appearing between the scaffolding and the building that it was supposed to be attached to. As the platform and I rapidly approached the point of no return my life flashed before my eyes. It wasn't quite as good as it was the first time, but it was better than most repeats on TV.

My options were limited: hold on to the lintel and die under a falling lump of oak, fall down the chasm and die, or summon every expletive that I have ever known and hurl them moronwards. I chose the latter. It worked, and the scaffold came back from the brink. I was shaken and very stirred, and now had two sheepish additions to the list of people never to be worked with again.

They have not, as far as I know, yet found out who is the heaviest.

Barn Free

Some people never learn. No matter how many times they bang their head against a brick wall, they just get up and do it again. I have to admit that I fit right in to the vanguard of the stupid, never-learning band of perennial optimists. My latest fall relates to a barn re-renovation that has come my way.

The house and barn was converted and renovated about three years ago. It was done on the cheap - that is, very badly. Every original feature was plaster-boarded over or rendered. It is my unenviable task to bring the warmth and character of the old building back for the new owners.

Things had been going remarkably smoothly: new window openings created and glazed, walls repointed, ceilings raised etc, etc... In fact things were going nearly too well. One major task left to do was to remove the extremely gash-glazed monstrosity that had been installed in what had been the enormous opening to the barn. The plan was to take out the old glazed frame and with all possible haste build up a new stone arch in its place. All of this done to the strictest possible time schedule to keep the bad weather out.

Knowing how long things take in France, I had taken the precaution of ordering the arch stonework back in August. Just three weeks ago I went to the quarry and was assured that I would have the arch by the middle of the next week. Full of optimistic bravado one slightly damp Monday morning, I set to work with a hammer and a chainsaw. Before the day was out there was a huge gaping hole in the front of the building where once there had been double-glazing - slightly leaky, but well capable of keeping out the very worst that could be thrown at it.

I tossed aside frivolous questions about when I was going to fill it back in again. I knew that I would have my arch in the next couple of days. Unfortunately, the next couple of days, even the next couple of weeks, failed to bring the slightest sign of anything arch-like coming my way. The only thing that has come my way is very well-deserved flak. Even the unisex, multi-racial, multi-national and multi-lingual workforce has been complaining about the draught. I don't really understand what they are complaining about. In fact, I don't really understand what they are saying most of the time, on account of one of them coming from Scotland, another from Ireland, and one from Marseille. Ironically, the one from Marseille - a slip of girl who is tiling the floors - is probably the easiest one to understand. She is something of a rarity in France, being a female artisan, and is usually made to feel rather uncomfortable by her fellow French artisans.

The English positive attitude to female workers is very much appreciated on site. Apparently, it makes a refreshing change from the 'woman know your place' philosophy that is still common currency over here. At one point, while Sue was helping me with the pointing and the tiler's friend was giving her a hand before going off to join the circus (yes, truly!), 50 per cent of the workforce was female. A not unpleasant situation and a small step in the right direction.

In the meantime, a huge green tarpaulin takes the place of a beautiful stone arch, draughts are replaced by a howling gale, but at least the fresh air is doing them good. Will I ever learn? All the evidence suggests not.

Wildcat

In a small town in the South West of France there is a little kitten by the name of Louis, who started last week as a boy and ended it as something different.

When he woke up on Friday morning he might well have looked back on the last few months of his short life.... the first six weeks that he spent living under a bush; the next six weeks that he spent living behind a futon after Sue rescued him from likely euthanasia by a farmer, his life changed from a wild, hissing and spitting feral beast to a loving lapcat.

As he sat there playing with his toy mice, wondering why he had not been fed, he had no inkling of what was about to befall him. He was to become a few grammes lighter, a little less tom, and a whole lot calmer.

Sue was rather anxious about his journey from boy to eunuch, I did my best to reassure her. I pointed out that he generally forgets that he has just been fed approximately two minutes after he has eaten, he cleans out his bowl and everybody else's and then cries out for more. Being half-Siamese, his cries can easily be heard on the dark side of the moon.

This phenomenal memory should mean that two hours after the chop, he would have absolutely no recall of any spherical objects ever having been attached to the back end of his body.

All went well, the deed was done, the vet was paid, the obligatory jokes made, and we brought him home. Unfortunately the anaesthetic was still having a bit of an effect on him: he came flying out of his cat carrier..... well, his front end attempted to, but his back end was not receiving the instructions. This led to a cat with front paws scrabbling and back legs flailing, looking like nothing so much as Lee Marvyn's drunken horse in Cat Ballou.

After some serious TLC from Sue he was fast asleep and entering fast recovery mode. True to form, he woke up this morning, howling for breakfast, completely oblivious to the fact that his tree would be missing a couple of baubles this Christmas.

Having made sure that he would not be contributing to cat overpopulation, our attention has turned to the once-overpopulated fish pond. We inherited half a dozen or so goldfish from the previous owners, but at its zenith this summer we counted at least 60 fish swimming happily amongst the frogs and toads. At the latest count, there were a mere six fish rattling around in an empty pond.

Either they have gone on a hike, we have acquired an alligator, or one of the cats has bought a fishing rod. Either way, we shall be spared the somewhat tedious task of sorting the boys from the girls and taking them to the vet's for a bit of keyhole surgery. In fact, go forth and multiply, my children, except you, Louis. You stay home and imagine what might have been. Have another biscuit and dream of mice. Or fish.

Chilled Out

Things are not really working out in the way that they were supposed to.

When I signed up for this whole moving to the South of France thing, I had visions that the summers would last forever, winter would never come and the cold would be something that you read about in an English newspaper.

In fact, I was so full of confidence when we first moved out here that I threw away all of my thermal underwear before leaving the UK. A decision that I was later to regret.

What I hadn't taken in to consideration is the simple geographical fact that continental landmasses get very hot in summer (result!), but what goes up must come down - and when it goes down, boy, does it go down.

In the last week we have passed from T-shirts to thermal long johns without passing go or collecting 200 Euros. Many of the leaves on the trees were still green up until last night. Today they took a unanimous decision to all fall off at the same time, although most of the trains still appear to be running.

They were running today, but they certainly weren't last Monday when there was yet another general strike in support of anti-privatisation or some such cause. Strikes are still very much a part of the working week over here, as they were back in the 1970s in the UK. A huge number of causes are considered strike-worthy, and it is generally thought to be most effective to strike on a Monday or a Friday (unless one of these days is a national holiday, in which case the strike should occur the day before, or the day after, thus ensuring a nice long weekend. Nothing furthers a fighting cause more than a well-rested worker).

I did briefly flirt with the idea of having a little strike myself, in order to show a bit of solidarity for the workers and all that. The idea was rather short lived, these things only really work when you are part of a bigger organisation. It would have been nearly as lonely as my self-employed Christmas works do. There is only a limited amount of fun to be had out of photocopying body parts when you are all alone.

This situation is one that is just changing. I have taken the brave step of doubling the workforce. Sue has now become an employee, in charge of office work with a liberal sprinkling of hard manual work thrown in. Her first day of employment coincided nicely with the national strike. Privatisation being something that she feels very strongly about on a Monday, this meant that there was no work forthcoming on her first day.

What goes around comes around, and as the thermometer sticks obstinately in the minus portion, I can see a nice little pointing job coming up - the sort of job that is out in the cold and needs that certain female touch.

Affairs of the Hearth

It all started so simply, with one of those typical phrases that clients throw at their builder. It's the sentence that strikes fear into the heart of the sturdiest artisan, the sentence that always begins with "Could you just......"

I feel sure that Michelangelo must have heard those self-same words when the ceiling of the Sistine chapel had just been plastered and was looking in need of a fresco or two.

I found myself on the receiving end of a "Could you just build me a fireplace with some of that old stone that you have outside?"

I had, of course, neglected to follow rule one - never leave any materials on site, somebody will always find something for you to do with them. Construct a Wendy house in the style of Salisbury cathedral out of that old scaffold plank... build a fireplace using that rough old pile of reject stone that doesn't have any faces or corners. You are always on a hiding to nowhere.

Unfortunately, hardened and cynical as I am towards clients (I can turn away work all day long) I had met my match with this lady client. Being a serial house buyer, she has met every kind of builder and picked up a few tricks along the way.

Before I could even begin to laugh at her request, she had followed through with flattery and compliments about my unparalleled skills as a master builder.

A flutter of eyelashes, a cup of tea, and I seemed to have got the contract, that I didn't think that I wanted.

It was just a simple fireplace to go around a wood-burning stove. I am absolutely certain that I heard the word 'simple', and I'm sure that the word 'small' was also used. Needless to say, as soon as I started setting out the base, widths got wider, heights got higher, and designs got grander.

Despite my constant protestations, the fireplace was growing into one that could quite comfortably seat four. Idi Amin could have barbecued every general in his army in it, and still had room to pitch a tent. Several tons of stone and a small beach of sand and cement later, the structure was up; it just lacked something. I felt certain that when the monolith was mooted, an off-the-shelf oak beam was included in the plan. But it would look so much nicer with an authentic old one.

Where was I to find an old beam at short notice? As luck would have it, I remembered running into a Frenchman who had offered to sell me some oak beams. The problem was that this was some months ago and I had scribbled his number on an old delivery note. Luckily Sue's filing system has a special place for such things. Phone calls were made, and a meeting arranged with a Spanish/Frenchman who was a cross between Grizzly Adams and an extra from Deliverance. After a quick visit to his yard, the beam was bought and loaded. The only thing left to do was to hoist it into place, and to see what the client thought of it. She declared that the somewhat rustic old beam was absolutely perfect and that she loved it.

All's well that ends well in this case. It's the exception that proves the rule. Next time I hear the words "Could you just..." I will run for the hills as fast as my little legs will carry me.

The Great French Labour Exchange

As far as deals go, it is not in the running for deal of the century. In fact, it is rather difficult to pin down exactly who are the winners and who are the losers.

Every year thousands of young, energetic and well-qualified French people, along with small business owners, get themselves a ticket on Eurostar and install themselves in the south east of England.

In exchange, France receives from the UK a hapless band of retirees, would-be builders, and young families who don't know or care where they are going so long as it is not back to the UK.

Besides these obvious differences, there is one major factor which separates these two parties: the state of their respective bank accounts. Most of the French will not have much behind them, and be hungry to start earning cash, or they will be looking to take their business into new realms of success. The Brits, on the other hand, may have run successful businesses, have pensions or, as mere members of the lumpen proletariat will have won on the great property lottery.

It is not rare to run into young Brits who barely know what a day's work is, but are more than capable of buying a property outright and look forward to never having to work for a living. This is generally their reward for having bought a house in the UK and just sat in it for a while.

If you surveyed the two parties, their respective incentives for the trans-Channel swap would probably come down to the French making a living and the Brits making a life. The French see the dynamism and pluralism of a thriving economic cherry that they want a bite at. The Brits see a reflection of an idyllic bygone era when things were not driven by the market economy.

The French find themselves in a thriving country where taxes are low, nobody closes for lunch, supermarkets are open 24 hours a day and are full of international products, jobs are plentiful and well paid, there are hardly any strikes, there are more workers than civil servants, the weather is terrible and there are people everywhere.

The Brits find themselves in a country with a dying economy that taxes businesses so heavily that most fail within three years, where unemployment is high and most people work for the state, strikes take place most weeks, houses are cheaper, there is plenty of room for everybody and the weather is much better.

In talking to the newly-landed Brits, you find a constantly recurring pattern. They always say that they wanted to escape from the rat race, to improve their lifestyle. With the next breath, they complain about the difficulty of getting anything done, or buying certain things.

They can't understand why no businesses want to make any money. It is simple: if they make money, they pay it all in tax, therefore they try not to make any money. Therefore, they close for a long lunch, they don't hurry, they don't overdevelop the land to sell for huge profits, they only sell enough local produce to tick along. This gives you the laid-back lifestyle that you wanted. I suspect that the Frenchman abroad finds exactly the reverse; this is why most of them plan to return to France after making their fortunes.

You pay your money and you take your choice.

Monsieur L'autobus

It appears that French bus drivers don't take holidays, or at least if they do, they don't drive to wherever their destination is.

This was the conclusion that I came to after visiting some of our French friends for a New Year mini-celebration. They had politely asked me if I had spent a relaxing and enjoyable holiday over the Christmas period; I tried to explain that I had merely taken 'a busman's holiday'.

They understood all of the words, and couldn't fault the order that they were put in. The vital missing element was what I meant. After a long and protracted explanation about how a bus driver ends up driving on his own holiday, realisation dawned and it was confirmed that no such expression exists in French. This is probably because no self-respecting Frenchman is daft enough to put himself out much during his holiday.

Leave that to the mad dogs and Englishmen. On Christmas Day I had to knock Santa out of the way so that I could continue tiling the hallway floor. His reindeer looked on in disgust and shook their heads at my crass behaviour....

Actually, it would be fair to say that Christmas is not celebrated very seriously in our house. Sue did manage to put up our elderly Woolworth's special genuine reusable tree, and she hung the tinsel and lights but they never did get plugged in.

The 11 Christmas cards gazed down upon the two presents beneath the tree.

I did actually crack this year and excelled myself by buying a present for Sue. I was not going to, but got hit by an overwhelming feeling of guilt on my last day at work. I was chatting to Guillaume, and I casually asked him if he and his wife bothered buying presents. He then launched into a diatribe about how important it is to buy and receive gifts. I felt meaner than Scrooge on a bad day and decided that I had to do something about it.

I left site early and headed in to Gaillac. This was the Friday just before Christmas, and my heart was full of dread at the thought of battling through the crowds. I needn't have worried; there was me, an old man and a dog and a couple of tumbleweed in the High Street.

The French economy is in pretty poor shape; this was confirmed by the shopkeepers that I spoke to, they all declared Christmas to have been a catastrophe. This could perhaps explain why the woman in the jewellers took the cash that I gave her in exchange for a rather attractive necklace and popped it straight into her purse without making the customary visit to the till.

No messy receipts or anything like that. She had obviously decided that the only way to make Christmas pay was by delving into the black economy. Anyway, Sue liked her gifts, the woman liked her cash and I had a thrilling time with the tiling. They say a change is as good as a rest - perhaps I could have a rest for a change next year.

Taxing Times

For some reason, best known to themselves, the French believe that the tax year ends on December 31 and not the April 5.

This rather puts a damper on the French New Year, which is heralded by cries of despair, attempted suicides, wailing and gnashing of teeth from those unfortunate enough to be self-employed on this fair continent.

For myself, it has seen the arrival of reams of forms to be filled in, courtesy of the illness people, the retirement people, the tax people, the employers of people people, the holidays for employees people, the medicals for employees people, the retirement for artists people.
I think they may have been having a laugh with the last one, but they do all share one common denominator. As soon as you fill in and send the form back, as sure as eggs are oeufs, you will get a stonking great big bill.

The French are rather proud of the fact that their income tax looks quite reasonably rated at a mere 20 per cent or thereabouts. You may wonder how they manage to run such a fantastic health service with no waiting lists, have excellent schools and subsidise all of their industry on a mere 20 per cent of our income. But, they don't.

Before you can even contemplate handing over your 20 per cent, you hand over 44 per cent of your income to the people who look after retirement, hospital and sick people.

More inroads are made into your wallet by the other bloodsuckers. The insurance people want a cut, as do the accountants, doctors and banks. When all of these people have finished savaging your near-lifeless corpse, they then throw your husk to the tax people, who pick the bones for whatever they can find.

This means that the happy and jolly artisan who had money to burn at the end of December finds himself nearly 80 per cent poorer by the end of January. Imagine Tiny Tim sent out into the cold at the end of January; no food, not even a stick to burn to keep himself warm, blisters on his shoeless feet, and a hacking cough as the first sign of consumption. This is the fate of the French artisan.

How much kinder to end the tax year at the beginning of April, when the trees are in bud, the sap is rising and summer is coming.

As we poor ex-pat builders struggle to learn the French tax system, we post some of the most entertaining end-of-year profits that you could imagine. My electrician friend actually earned less than £500 last year after paying all of his charges - only slightly less than he earned washing cars after school 25 years ago. The melancholy plumber was made more melancholy by his YTS-level income.

As for me, the money I turned over would keep the economy of a small country afloat, and at the end of it I look likely to take home less money than I did in 1988. Do I begrudge what I am paying for? No way. Next week I am going to retire sick, to a hospital school, ask for a subsidy and claim it all back on the insurance.

Pied dans la Bouche

You can take me anywhere. You can take me anywhere twice. The second time is usually a sheepish visit to apologise for the first.

This is most usually true of the dreaded dinner party. Eating at the home of friends, acquaintances, or almost complete strangers is the mainstay of the social life of an English person living in the quieter corners of the back end of beyond.

We are not heavily distracted in these parts by multiplexes, pubs, international restaurants, theatres and all those other trappings of the 21st century. The trappings of the 19th century are more our thing: the art of good conversation - intelligence, wit, enjoying the company of others - in short, the dinner party.

We don't get invited to many. I believe that this is simply because of our vegetarian leanings. I am sure that there are hundreds of people who would gladly pay for the privilege of my sparkling wit at their dinner table. The only thing holding them back is their carnal desires. (I think I mean carnivorous.)

It was with some excitement that we received an invitation to dinner last Saturday. The hosts were an Irish couple of a similar age to ourselves. He is a former window dresser, animation background painter, a would-be builder and soon-to-be-struggling artist who is married to an ex-mortgage arranger/narcoleptic life coach who is struggling with personal motivation.

It seemed like it could be fun. We duly arrived with gateau in hand (in the box that we bought it in, actually) and a bottle of wine. That bottle of wine was to be my undoing. There was an extra person and various children present, introductions were made and a cork popped. That cork popping was a problem - this was one of those rare occasions that I wasn't driving, and was therefore most definitely drinking.

I think that things were going quite well through the starter and main course. I was talking to the lady next to me about living in France; the wine was flowing. It was not my fault somebody pushed one of my buttons and got me talking about things that irritate me.

Besides disliking all people in general, I reserve particular disdain for the Walter Mitty ex-pats who leave their UK job in middle management to reinvent themselves as a former rocket scientist turned master builder, architect, interior designer, project manager. I can talk for hours on the subject. Everybody must have been enjoying my razor wit, because all other conversations stopped. I held the floor.

Sue was much too far away to kick me beneath the table, so how was I supposed to know that the person next to me was an ex journalist who has reinvented herself as an interior design project manager? Our hosts' reinvention had unfortunately also been filtered out of my consciousness by wine, and there was definitely no way that I could have known about the insurance claim.

I hate all things insurance - having it, paying it, claiming, and people who claim and push up the premiums. I could not feasibly have known that she had recently claimed a million Euros from her insurance company.

Oh well, I had a great time. I must remember next time, to keep Sue within kicking distance, and maybe to mix some water with the wine. If there is a next time, that is.

Blanc Out

A packet of dried prunes, a copy of a history of Europe the size of a large housebrick, five bored and complaining cats, and a view that has ceased to exist more than five feet away from the house. Not everybody's dream of an idyllic Sunday breakfast in the sunny South of France.

Warm croissants and the sun reflecting off far-flung snow capped peaks may be more like it. Currently, we have one of those elements: the snow, and boy, do we have the snow.

It came in yesterday morning, started to settle, snowed some more, then some more, and then decided not to stop. By midday any hope of leaving the property was lost. By mid-afternoon, any hope of finding vehicles left outside was also lost.

Approximately two feet of snow fell yesterday, and the consequences have been serious and far-reaching. The satellite dish has been covered, unless a suicide slide onto the roof is made, we are condemned to re-watch old films on DVD - or even worse, work our way through all 57 episodes of The Professionals that Sue keeps for emergencies. All trips to the tabac to pick up a newspaper are hopeless, hence the ploughing through of the history book.

The biggest single catastrophe is the cancellation of the Sunday trip to the veg market. Being vegetarian, the prospect of the next week spent without fruit and veg is even less appealing than it might be to most of our neighbours. The snow also means no pastries for breakfast and absolutely no fresh bread to go with the warming soup made from the fresh veg from the market that we can't go to.

We have been furiously burning anything burnable in our Norwegian wood burner. Any dead and dying trees have gone up in smoke, as have all the old beams and off-cuts that come my way in my daily travels. All of the old tongue and groove panelling that we stripped off the walls has nearly gone.

The cats were briefly under the misapprehension that snow was fun; this was soon dispelled when they discovered that their paws disappeared and their pendulous bellies dragged on the freshly fallen snow, leading to mild feelings of chill. They have since taken to hogging the fire and drawing any warmth possible from vulnerable parts of our bodies - that is when they are not whingeing about how hungry they are and how awful is their lot.

There are, of course, huge and positive benefits to a covering of snow. The scenery, when the weather lifts for five minutes, is achingly beautiful and our piles of rubble, unkempt garden, and all the multitude of jobs to do in the garden are hidden by a deep and even blanket.

Huddling around a stove of burning debris is infinitely preferable to frostbite. The prunes are keeping me wonderfully regular, and my knowledge of late 19th century economics and politics has expanded beyond my wildest dreams - and what wild dreams they were!

Even Bodie and Doyle are starting to appeal, or is that just the first symptoms of cabin fever? Dig us out when spring comes, or when the prunes run out.

No Pain, No Gain

Pain is a wonderful thing for concentrating the mind. As I stood there in the middle of our garage/soon to be cinema (perhaps, take the word 'soon' with a pinch of salt), a rusty Stanley knife in one hand, and four intact knuckles on the other, I was hard-pressed to think of anything that was worrying me, other than my immediate pain.

The fifth knuckle was now a flap of skin, barely holding on and starting to leak heavily. The main thing running through my head was that familiar phrase known to the accident prone, 'I wish that I could make that, didn't happen'. This is always the precursor to the pain to come, and come it did.

At that moment in time, I was not in the slightest bit worried about my non-existent bank balance. I couldn't have cared a fig that the French state was spending beyond its means and relying on me to prop it up single handedly. All I cared about was stemming the flow, and trying to fix it. I ran into the house and called for Sue to administer first aid. I don't want you to think that she leads a sedentary life, but I did have to wake her up. This was at 5.30 in the afternoon.

Being a frequent visitor to accident city, I assessed it to be a wound that we could handle ourselves, given a first aid kit. Luckily, we have one of those vorsprung durch technik cars, and with typically Teutonic efficiency they supply a comprehensive operating kit along with the front seat. Sue retrieved the said kit from the car and set about opening it.

We could probably have dealt with a major international incident with the contents. There were blankets, creams, bandages, scissors, plasters and sealed packets too numerous to mention. After 20 minutes of playing with every toy in the toy box, I was patched up and deemed fit to return to work.

The pain in that knuckle was soon forgotten the next day - the minus six temperature was enough to persuade the skin on my thumb to split and open the parts that are supposed to be below the skin to the outside world. Things couldn't really get much worse.

The plus side was that I was not worrying at all about the difficulties of making a living, the huge tax bill that I had just received was not even registering on the Botherometer.

As I unhitched the trailer, I was not thinking about the high level of unemployment, I wasn't worrying at all about ethnic tensions in the inner cities. I was just glad that the scaffolding planks that we put at the rear of the trailer made the trailer jump apart from the ball hitch. This would have made a terrible clanging noise when the coupling hit the metal at the back of the van, if it hadn't been for the fortunate positioning of my finger between the two.

A perfect excuse to use my own first aid kit. As I sit here throbbing, attempting to type with a mere 70 per cent digit effectiveness, I can't help thinking that I'm sure that there was something bothering me. I'm blowed if I can remember what it was.... aargh, the pain.

Spring 2006

Artistic Licence

Not so long ago, wealthy families who cast out their black sheep put them on a ship France. Once the ne'er-do-well landed he would make his way to Paris, find himself a garret, buy a set of paintbrushes, and starve to death.

Well, in fact it would be a race to see whether the starvation would get to him before the absinthe had a chance to rot away his brain and disintegrate his vital organs.

This was all very noble. It got rid of unwanted relatives, kept a few backstreet cafes in business, and even produced the odd bit of artwork into the bargain.

Things have changed. It seems that you no longer have to come from a fabulously wealthy background to become an artist. Anybody can do it, even the working classes. One thing has not changed. They still come to France.

Their reasons are many - the fabulous scenery, the light, the spare building that could be converted into a studio if only there was an artist to fill it. I have lost track of the number of times that I have stood looking at a beautiful but quite useless huge area of barn, and listened while the owner has told me about his dream of opening an art school. If every one of these dreams came to fruition there would be approximately two schools for every potential pupil. There are so many artists, and potential artists, flocking to this area that some villages count 50 per cent of their population as being artists. Some hamlets are closer to the 100 per cent mark.

This does of course lead to some colourful characters. I have seen one version of the standard cape-clad, fedora-wearing archetype with a huge booming voice; he was an American. I know an Irishman from the lower reaches of society, who will only paint scenes from the local town of Gaillac. He will not contemplate painting anywhere else. When pressed upon his future plans after he has painted every building in the town, he thinks that he may have to start all over again. I know a Belgian girl who paints string. If she can't actually get hold of any string, she will paint something else and make it look like string. She also paints black-eyed peas, corks, lichen, and anything else that is intricate, time-consuming, painstaking and likely to turn any sane person into an axe-wielding psychopath.

These people are actual, genuine, struggling artists, desperate to succeed in their chosen field, and make a living. A less generous person might see them as desperate to not have to get a proper job. They are, of course, accompanied, and outnumbered by the droves of middle class dabblers, who find themselves with too much money, too much time, too little purpose in life, and too little talent. Any trip to a local art show will yield an embarrassment of riches.... eccentric perspective, wobbly lines, poorly-mixed colours, and all at a vibrant price.

What place is there for these people in the local economy, in a country where there is a dearth of people to maintain and repair things? I suppose if you can't find anybody to fix that crack in your wall, you could cover it with a picture. If your trousers fell down and you needed a piece of string, you could always unpick a painting. What price art?

Troughs and Peaks

Sometimes it appears that life really can't get much worse. The bank balance has once again shrunk to zero, the taxman is making even more outrageous demands (he will generally stop short of demanding both kidneys, one will do), the winter is never-ending, and everything is a mess. It can appear to be not really worth the effort of putting oneself through the struggle of yet another week of thankless toil against the rock face.

That is, until you get out of bed on a Monday morning, have a cup of tea, tiptoe outside to warm the van up to defrost the windscreen. Miracle of miracles: no frost.... this can mean only one thing. You drive to work with baited breath, awaiting the dawn. You pass through the village of Cordes, sneak a peak at the wonderfully modern digital thermometer in the town square. YES! It reads zero. That means that the temperature is going to rise into single digits. Oh joy.

Things get better, the sun is rising over the vineyards, the sky is clear. Surprise, when I touch the pile of sand with my shovel, it actually slides in, like a knife through butter - the first time in two-and-a-half months that the shovel hasn't clanged and bounced off the frozen heap.

It is a Monday morning and things are going frighteningly well. We are pointing the front of the building that we have been waiting so long to attack. This means that we are within an ace of finishing the job, taking down the scaffolding, and getting paid.

We have even advanced far enough to reward ourselves with a tea break. The customer passes me a letter to translate. It is from the hôtel des impôts (tax office). I read it, read it again, and confirm his worst suspicions. It is a bill.

Actually, the word 'bill' does not really describe it. It is more of a polite kind of extortion. I have been at the receiving end of a few too many of these lately. But even to a jaded palate such as mine, this was an eye waterer. It was a simple seven-page document demanding a payment of 177,000 Euros within 30 days (about £120,000). It had come to him via the UK, so that his 30 days were nearly up. There is nothing like seeing somebody else in the mire up to the nose, when yours is only up to the chin, to make life suddenly seem rosier.

We piled back to work, pointed up the house. More miracles, the French doors that we had been waiting so long for arrived. They were installed, sealing up the house that had been at the mercy of the elements for so many months.

I occasionally glimpsed the client wandering about absorbed in a small cloud of joy. His house was pointed, his lounge was finally sealed against the bitter wind, he had a bill, he was no longer haemorrhaging heat. He also had a bill. Who cares about the bill? The job was done, the workmen were leaving, he couldn't pay us quick enough.

People are so thrilled when the builders arrive, but they don't know true joy until we leave. I would still like to believe, of course, that it was a tear of sadness that I saw in his eye from the rear-view mirror.

Accidents Will Happen

We all have our own little weaknesses. Some people sneeze when they see a cat - my particular weakness is dirt. I only have to walk past somebody who is repairing a car, and I am covered in oil.

My friend and erstwhile colleague Guillaume is particularly susceptible to potential accident situations. He finds it physically impossible to walk away from the possibility of an accident without taking part. I once made the mistake of telling him a short story of how I had once dented a car. Two hours later, he finished telling me about the list of cars that he had written off, covering every offering from the French motor industry of the last 30 years, to a story about rolling a car down a snow-covered hillside until it became lodged against a rock just above a sheer drop.

Having worked alongside the man who cut through a plank that he was stood upon, just before falling to the lower floor and breaking several bones in his foot, I can guarantee that the stories are true.
Unfortunately, I was working on the other side of the building when he became fascinated by the tile hoist. This is a ladder-type affair with a cable and motor that sends a small skip of roof tiles up and onto the roof. It looked like more fun than a walk up a ladder. I'm sure that it was, as he perched on the little skip admiring the scenery, until the cable snatched, jerked, and tipped him southwards. Luckily, his fall

was broken by the ground, which left him with nothing more serious than a twisted ankle. He did at least have the decency to be a little sheepish as he explained what he had done.

I was not best pleased, my reasons being twofold. I would not particularly relish the task of telling his newly-widowed bride that she would have to develop a taste for Scotch Whisky as her husband would no longer be attacking the optics.

Secondly, a serious accident in France generally involves a swift visit from the gendarmes, closely followed by a leisurely time for reflection behind bars. As an entrepreneur, you are considered to have caused the death of an employee by exploiting them in a callously capitalist way, and thus deserving of a prompt and severe punishment. The general advice in such situations is to run for the hills. There is a very good reason why the Foreign Legion came in to being in France.

Having recovered from his twisted ankle, Guillaume decided to remove the prop from beneath the chimney. The chimney did not fall on his head, but the plank of wood between the chimney and the prop did. A trip to the doctor and half a dozen stitches soon sorted that out - the saving grace being the huge white bandage that the doctor wrapped over the top of his head and beneath his chin half a dozen times. Every site needs a cartoon image of a bandaged man to raise morale.

All of these accidents beg one question during the telling. The listener can always see what is going to happen - so why can't Guillaume?

Cinema Paradiso

Sooner or later, if you lie down with dogs you are going to catch fleas. It has happened to me. I have spent years working with barking mad clients and architects who have no idea of the practical but plenty of ideas of the fantastical, and they have finally given me a bad dose of metaphorical fleas.

Having just reached the end of our home renovation, what have I done? Sat back on the sofa and taken a well-deserved break? Nice idea. Decided to drop things down a gear or two and enjoy my achievements?

How can anybody possibly sit still when there is a half-finished garage attached to the side of their house?

The previous owner had decided to build a garage on a steep slope, on solid rock. The door being at the lowest point, this meant that the only vehicle capable of entering the garage was a four-wheel drive with crampons fitted, or a tank. Owning neither, we decided that it could be a great idea to change the garage into a room of some description. Having a look around the rest of the house, it soon became apparent that we had all of the rooms that you traditionally need. We have bathrooms, bedrooms etc. About the only rooms that we don't have is a dining room and a gym. Nobody ever uses a dining room for anything other than storing an unused dining room table, and exercise is purely for the bored and uninteresting.

It was time to think laterally, and stupidly. I have heard nearly every stupid suggestion known to man: taking the roof off to form a covered terrace, taking down the front and building a stone arch based around the length of a pair of curtains. Nobody has ever asked me to build a cinema. Eureka! That was the one for me.

Before I could even draw a breath, the garage door was off, blockwork was going up, cables were being laid and concrete being poured.
The flurry of construction has led me to the point of needing technology. It is impossible to build a film projector with stone and a hammer and chisel, so I have had to outsource this one. This need for things from the modern world necessitated a trip to our nearest city of Toulouse. I have been there once before; I didn't like it much, too many people. But sometimes in this life we all have to make sacrifices, and this was mine. Armed with magazine articles, Sue by my side, and our good friends Guillaume and Catherine with their heavy metal-obsessed teenage daughter, off we went to the big city.

I rediscovered a few half-remembered truths: you will generally end up buying the first thing that you see, and electronics shop assistants are trained to speak to you as if you are a complete cretin. Several hours, and several insulting diatribes from spotty techno morons later, I had what I needed. We have the technology, we have the building, we have a daft idea, all we need is some popcorn.

People Power

I love people. I am truly, what is often referred to as a 'people person', in much the same way as Charles Manson was. I do stop just short of shooting and dismembering my fellow bipeds, but that is not to say that the thought never occurs to me.

My lack of patience, empathy and compassion is not the greatest of assets when dealing with clients in the heady world of property renovation.

Customers are demanding. They need constant reassuring and hand-holding, they need to be told that a mud-filled stinking pit will one day be a beautiful modern kitchen that Raymond Blanc would be proud of. Sometimes I can do it, if I put my mind to it. I can be very good at it, I can be charming - I just don't feel like it most of the time. Working with the French has taught me a great deal about anger management, or in my case, surliness management. You don't have to manage it, just let it out. A Frenchman is never backwards in coming forwards when it comes to letting people know if they have annoyed him. He doesn't doff his cap and say thank you very much, he lets loose a tirade of invectives.

Take this morning. I have been constructing a sun terrace on stilts at the side of a house. It is a fairly complex operation. The client is too mean to pay an architect and has left me to do all of the design. The piles have been sunk into the rock; the concrete beams have been poured. He comes out this morning (not my best time of day, I just want to get on with the job), and says that he thinks that the terrace is six inches too small. He is worried about walking around his table. There was a time when I would have just taken it on the chin, got my head down and seethed inside. Not today. He now knows what size his terrace is remaining at, what size it will never be, what I think about unhelpful comments after the fact, and exactly what he can do with his tape measure. I felt loads better for it; he didn't, as he scuttled back into his hutch. This gave me the chance to shout and swear about him in French with my colleague.

I believe that everybody should learn a second language when they are halfway through their life. It completely refreshes a jaded palate. There is a joy in forming the new words and spitting them out, venting anger and frustrations. The fun is probably increased because it never fails to make the French laugh. They are obviously pointing at me and saying 'Listen to the daft Englishman swearing in our language.' I don't care it makes me feel good.

The strange outcome of my new Gallic behaviour is that people actually treat you better the worse you behave. This mornings' client came out with a cup of tea and a cheque after my tirade. When I was nice and polite they used to ignore me and never bothered paying their bills.

We shall see what client nonsense tomorrow brings, but if you hear about an axe murder in the south west of France, you will know that I had just cause - six inches, my foot.

Driving Forwards

Deserted roads, sweeping bends, breathtaking scenery across sheer drops, vineyards as far as the eye can see.....

Sounds idyllic, doesn't it? Echoes of a bygone age? Well, yes it can be. It can give you that almost-worth-being-alive feeling in the morning. It can raise you when you are low, and it can also very nearly be your undoing.

When I was working up in that big smoke people know as London, I had to do a lot of driving from site to site. The boredom of being sat in an endless queue of traffic on Mitcham Common was alleviated by the radio and that finest of British traditions, the packed lunch. I could quite happily sit in my van, unpack my sandwiches, pour a cup of tea from my Thermos, place it on the dashboard and eat and drink in perfect peace, only interrupted by the occasional forward movement. Lunch on the move - at between one and one and a half miles per hour.

Things are not quite the same in the jolly old south west of France.

Just the other day I found myself in the middle of one of my messier days. I was concreting in the morning - not conducive to stopping for meals, because your work literally gets harder the longer that it takes you. Directly after that, I had to run around from left to right picking up doors, stone and all those other things that you need to start the next job.

This necessitated a rolling lunch - surely not too much of a problem as lunch was to be the traditional sandwich affair (cheese as normal, as they have been every day for very nearly 20 years now). This may sound a little dull, but just over three years ago I made the transfer from Cheddar to French cheese. I am nothing if not adventurous.

Lunch would have been a huge success, except for one thing. I appear to have become French in my way of driving. This means that I take to the road at the maximum possible speed. This can impact the sandwich box against the back of the seat, spilling the contents. There is generally nobody else on the roads, but if somebody else should have the temerity to be in front of me I have no choice but to overtake them. I found myself starving hungry, glancing at the sandwich beside me but unable to grab it as I had one hand on the wheel and the other desperately shuffling the gears as I tried to overtake a small Citroen van.

(When did I suddenly become this maniacal overtaker? I'm not entirely sure.)

Once I was clear of my obstacle, I thought that maybe this was sandwich time. No such luck - too many bends. Lots of bends on generally empty roads leads to very sloppy driving. There are not very many white lines and no cats' eyes so you tend to take most bends on a kind of middle-of-the-road basis. This is all very well until you meet that occasional vehicle coming the other way. Flashing lights, blaring horns, burning rubber, drainage ditches and sheer drops all conspire to rather ruin your lunch.

Now I finally begin to understand why all of the French sit down at a restaurant for lunch. It is part of the natural selection process. Those that sit still survive and live to eat another day. Those that don't, crash - or very nearly.

The Apprentice

It seems to me that life is often an almost continuous unbroken line of small errors..... much like the white line that I crossed when I overtook that slow-moving small blue car.

Unfortunately, the contents of the car turned out to be a small blue gendarme, who proceeded to give me a not-very-pleasant on-the-spot-fine.

I was happily on my way home to do a spot of electrical wiring - not perhaps the best idea that I have ever had, as it turned out. Everything seemed to go swimmingly well - all of the electric points worked, the spotlights even came on in the new bar area. The problem came when I turned the spots off. There was a small bang and everything went suddenly very dark - another small error.

A quick phone call (one where I had to eat a small slice of humble pie and listen to an excessively gloating electrician friend) soon sorted things out.

The electricity fiasco soon cleared away any thoughts that I might have had about connecting up the new radiators myself. This was a job for Pat the melancholy plumber. His new girlfriend is still keeping away the melancholia, but only just.

He dutifully turned up today with his faithful sidekick Jacques and a gawky youth in a boiler suit. The youth turned out to be a work experience apprentice with all of the standard teenage attributes; feet too big, expression too bored and apparent deafness.

I am being generous by suggesting deafness, because that is the kindest explanation for him handing Jacques a screwdriver when asked for a spanner, then a pair of pliers, and then finally a spanner - the wrong size, but a spanner none the less. His feet came into their own when they sensed a bucket of water in the vicinity; this was soon spread to all four corners of the room.

It is a little bit of a chicken-and-egg question as to whether the young apprentices get treated like morons because they behave like morons, or they behave like that because of the way they are treated. In the UK, apprentices are generally used for their comedy value - sent to the builders' merchants for a long weight (wait - ha ha), a skirting board ladder or a tin of tartan paint.

In France, they are there in order to worship at the altar of the artisan. They can watch. They may be allowed to pass things. But they must never do anything useful.

I have seen many a maçon working with his apprentice. The maçon will stand around doing nothing while his apprentice serves him with materials. The apprentice then has to stand around while the maçon places his block in position. This is not an efficient use of manpower.

You could train a monkey to lay blocks under supervsion in half a day, but that is not what it is all about. It is about knowing your place. And I have learnt my place. When driving on the right, if you observe a solid white line to your left, do not cross it, and you may finish the day a good 90 Euros richer.

Strike One

The French are revolting, once again. Springtime, the promise of warmer weather, and the need for longer weekends has once again brought the idea of striking back to the forefront of the Gallic consciousness.

The latest cause for nationwide grievance is the wholly unreasonable legislation that the Government is trying to introduce on behalf of the ogres known as the employers.

The basic thrust of the legislation is that if a business takes on an apprentice for a two-year period and they turn out to be a numbskull with the manual dexterity of a goldfish wearing mittens, the employer should be able to fire them without filling out three trees' worth of paper and a visit to the court of human rights.

The French like things the way that they are. A job is not seen as a by-product of a successful business. It is a basic human right and should be sacrosanct. If you start to sack people because they are not any good at their job, where will it all end?

Don't forget that the vast majority of the working population work for the state. They have a job for life, with a strict promotion scale based on existence more than performance.

I recently read about a gendarme who rather skilfully engineered his family planning in such a way that his generous paternity-leave enabled him to only work for two years in 10, allowing him to write a biography of The Beatles and work his way up to inspector based on theoretical years served.

The next day of national strikes is planned for next Tuesday. Funny that it should fall on a Tuesday. I'm sure that it has nothing to do with the fact that most workplaces are not open on a Monday, hence giving the righteous striker a nice long weekend.

In fairness, most workplaces cannot be opened on a Monday because their workers are only allowed to work a 35-hour week. If you let them in to work on a Monday they will have finished their week by Thursday.

Not all of the French support the strikes. Some people see them as ridiculous, but their voice is small. The general consensus seems to be that a change would be a good thing for France, but as France is extremely conservative, despite being socialist, things probably would not change.

France can look forward to a long summer of things grinding to a halt, useless apprentices keeping their jobs, very long weekends down in the country, and every chance that things will stay exactly as they are. Which country was it that invented the guillotine and started a revolution? Perhaps they don't want another one.

Bums on Seats

The imminent arrival of my 40th birthday (please don't send cash in the post, cheques will do fine) has hastened domestic building projects along at an alarming rate.

The once-derelict garage has been made over, and then some. Where once there was rubble and discarded sanitary ware, there is now a fully equipped cinema capable of projecting life-size images on the wall, and a surround sound system that could scare your unwanted elderly relatives half to death.

The grand opening is going to be the aforementioned birthday bash. Sue has it in mind that the room will be just perfect for dancing in. In preparation she has sifted through our entire music collection and distilled them into six or seven CDs guaranteed to bore you, annoy you, or delight you, depending on the direction you are looking at the 35-45 age bracket from.

For myself, I shall be content to watch the collection of Kylie videos and the director's cut of Apocalypse Now, followed by the Girls Aloud videos.

Others may mock my shallowness, but I would argue that there is no point in building a room with a huge screen unless you are going to fill it with aesthetically-pleasing images. What is more aesthetically pleasing to a rapidly middle-ageing man than beautiful young women singing and dancing?

Why have we done this, and how long did it take? We did it because we could, and it was six weeks from pouring the floor to the very first screening. Six weeks of punishing evenings and weekends, boosted by the odd rainy day off work, in order to install ceilings, walls, cupboards, tiles, doors and all the other paraphernalia. Not much fun at the time, but more than worth it in hindsight.

Of course, another principal reason for building it is because the life of an ex-pat, especially in winter, does tend to revolve around the DVD collection.

The almost complete unwatchability of French television (it is even worse that British TV, if you can believe that) renders box sets of long-vanished TV programmes extremely valuable. We have sat through hours, if not days of MASH, The Professionals and nearly every comedy that you care to mention. People have been known to commit minor felonies for a box set of The Sopranos and there is even a rumour that somebody has the whole first series of Lost. A bit too recent for me, perhaps.

The cinema does have a few unexpected side-effects. We were working close to home yesterday so I invited Guillaume, my colleague, back to the house for lunch. He was okay until we showed him the cinema. In order to show it working we put on the Girls Aloud video. Within 30 seconds he was lost. He screamed like a girl when I said that we had to go back to work. After three 'Just one mores', we made our way back, but he was still so dazed that he very nearly crashed the mini digger into the swimming pool.

One Frenchman nearly drowned, one Englishman very happy. And did I mention that it is my birthday soon?

Le Pub

Friday night in the pub; a couple of beers, a few mates, a scouse landlord, and a pub quiz.

You might be forgiven for thinking that it could only happen in the UK. Think again. After three years of yearning for a pint of lukewarm beer, we discovered the answer to all of our prayers hidden away not 10 minutes away from our house.

It is an actual, genuine, English-style pub, right in the middle of rural France and not anywhere near any particularly concentrated areas of thirsty ex-pats.

The landlord had apparently fled from the Liverpool health service for a new life in France. Having no useful transferable skills he settled upon the idea of trying a pub. However, he had obviously attended the same school of customer care and relations that I went to, which renders his suitability for the meet-and-greet world of public hospitality in the same league as Harold Shipman as a Help the Aged representative. He is so disdainful of customers that the pub doesn't even have a sign outside declaring that it is in fact a pub. It is so anonymous that we had passed it a dozen times before we even knew it was there.

As soon as we discovered it, we made ourselves at home, stopping off on a Friday night for a beer after work. The somewhat unpleasant landlord's discomfort at having to deal with yet another customer just added to the pleasure of a pint. For a bit of extra fun we ask him for a bowl of peanuts.

If you can believe what he says, he barely scrapes a living from running the pub. Any suggestions that attracting more customers to the pub might be a good thing, in that it would increase revenue, are met by a scowl. You can see his mind processing the thought of all those new people that he would have to be rude to. But, economic necessities being what they are, he occasionally has to succumb to punter-attracting measures. This takes the form of the pub quiz.

This is a bilingual affair. The local French have taken to the bizarre ways of the English and come along to play the game. It generally takes a long time to get started, because there is all the kissing to be got out of the way first. The pub is in the Aveyron, so a greeting takes the form of three kisses instead of the normal two - an increase of 33 per cent (or maybe 50 per cent?)

Unlike an English pub in England, you can't just slink in and plonk yourself down, you have to greet everybody who is already there; loads of shaking hands and kissing. In tests I have discovered that it best to arrive early. You still have to shake or kiss the same number of people, but at least they come to you.

Last Friday night saw us in the pub for the quiz, teamed up with an English ex-copper and his Finnish wife. In spite of my presence on the team we managed to answer more questions correctly than anybody else and came first. The best thing about our placing was the fact that the landlord was obliged to buy us a round of drinks as a prize. His face was a picture, and the arsenic didn't seem to affect the flavour of the beer too much.

Roaring Forties

Somehow, despite collapsing scaffoldings, falling rocks and a hundred other mishaps that the construction industry can throw at a body, I appear to have entered my fourth decade. As is only to be expected, I entered it not with a whimper but with a sizeable bang.

The bang was provided by a motley collection of nearly half a hundred English and French waifs and strays that were coerced into forming a birthday party.

Invitations had been sent out and supplies purchased. The invites all stipulated a starting time of 7.30pm. This was strictly observed by all of the French contingent - they all arrived within a space of 10 minutes, starting at 3 minutes before kick-off. The English approach to timekeeping was somewhat more haphazard: the last arrivals pitched up some time after the 10th jug of punch was making its rounds and any chance of being able to tell the time had been lost.

The punch helped to loosen the atmosphere. Jean-Paul, the electrical white goods supplier was happily chatting away in near fluent Scottish to Stuart the painter. Pascal, the Franco-German one-woman whirlwind, stopped just short of dancing on the tables and entertained the troops with cries of "Bloody Nora, who do you think I am, the Queen?" One does wonder where she learned the phrase. Having said that, my two phrases in German translate as 'The flowers are in the vase' and 'Your mother works in the oldest profession'. A little education can be dangerous thing.

Sue had organised the music, and was rather upset when it was criticised. This criticism soon turned to appreciation as the night wore on and the level in the jugs descended. She found herself a young lad to dance with, but unfortunately he was something of a walking catastrophe. Well, more of a falling catastrophe than anything else. He fell onto the dance floor before falling down the small stairwell. He would still be there now if he hadn't have held on so tightly to Sue's hand.

Elsewhere, the man who reputedly arrested Lord Archer (an act worthy of eternal approbation, if not an MBE) was sporting a violently pink jumper that should have got him arrested, or at least reprimanded. I decided against telling him about his sartorial misdemeanour on account of his wife being a top-flight barrister. I needn't have worried; it seems she does sex and death, not defamation.

The artists talked about art, the builders talked about anything but building. Most of what the builders said was unintelligible; no change there.

I managed to have my Girls Aloud moment. A group of us managed to watch a few videos on the cinema screen in reverential silence, broken only by one of the guests bursting in to see what the attraction was. He turned around and went straight back out again, in disgust. Not really his thing.

Luckily, we had an author of natural history books on hand when a moth the size of a First World War biplane landed on the glasses of our resident French teacher. "That'll be a male Emperor moth," he casually remarked as everybody else screamed and ran for cover.

The later hours of Sunday saw a much older and still no wiser Trevor moving about with great caution so as not to disturb that delicate head part of his body. Who said that getting older is no fun? I'm beginning to look forward to 50.